Susanna Wesley

Susanna Wesley

Susanna Wesley

Arnold A. Dallimore

BAKER BOOK HOUSE
Grand Rapids, Michigan 49516

© 1993 by Arnold A. Dallimore

Published by Baker Book House
P.O. Box 6287, Grand Rapids, Michigan 49516-6287

This edition produced in cooperation with
Evangelical Press, 12 Wooler Street, Darlington,
Co. Durham, DL1 1RQ, England. Original title: *Susanna*

Printed in the United States of America

Library of Congress Cataloging-in-Publication Data

Dallimore, Arnold A.
    Susanna Wesley / Arnold A. Dallimore.
       p.   cm.
    Includes bibliographical references and index.
    ISBN 0-8010-3018-8
    1. Wesley, Susanna Annesley, 1670–1742. 2. Anglicans—England—Biography.
3. Wesley, John, 1703–1791—Family. I. Title.
    BX8495.W55D35 1993
    287'.092—dc20
    [B]   92-41948

Contents

Preface

In writing this book it has been my aim to present a simple, readable account of the life of Susanna Wesley. I have tried to slant it especially towards women readers. I have provided a brief account of her background, her girlhood and her marriage to Samuel Wesley. I have gone on to show a number of traits of her husband's character: the two sides of his personality, his scholarly learning and clerical activities, together with his domineering manner and Susanna's patience in bearing it. We also see how the fact that he was constantly in debt cast a shadow over his life and that of his family.

Since Susanna left no diary or daily journal the only record we have from her pen is found in her letters. These I have quoted frequently. But the letters of her husband and her children also shed much light on her life and therefore I have often drawn on their correspondence in the pages before us.

I have made particular use of an account that Samuel wrote depicting the first thirty years of his life and which I refer to as his *Autobiography*. The original is in the possession of the Bodleian Library, Oxford University. It is in Samuel's handwriting and is very difficult to read. I have deciphered it all and it provides facts about his youth and his life as a young man that have not been mentioned by previous writers. I express my thanks to the Bodleian Library for photocopying this document for me.

For the first time in a biography of any of the Wesleys Samuel's action in leaving Susanna for nearly half a year is fully reported, as is also the way in which he forced their brilliant and beautiful daughter Hetty into marriage with an ignorant and boorish man. The former of these events is documented by Susanna's letters written at the time, and the latter by Hetty's letters and poems.

I express my thanks to Dr Frank Baker, the Editor in Chief of the Oxford edition of the *Works of John Wesley*, for the help he has given me, particularly with regard to the Hetty Wesley affair. I am grateful also to Mr D. W. Riley, M.L.A., Keeper of Printed Books at the John Rylands University, Manchester, England. This library now houses the Methodist archives, from which Mr Riley has provided me with various copies of correspondence by the Wesley family.

This book is sent forth with the desire that it may not only bring Susanna Wesley to the attention of many people, but that the story of her life may move many to copy her example of prayerfulness, patience and piety.

Arnold A. Dallimore
Cottam, Ontario, Canada

A portrait of Susanna Wesley which hangs
in the Epworth Old Rectory

The mother of John Wesley was evidently a woman of extraordinary power of mind. She was the daughter of Dr Annesley, a man well known to readers of Puritan theology as one of the chief promoters of the Morning Exercises. From him she seems to have inherited the masculine sense and strong decided judgement which distinguished her character.

(J. C. Ryle, *Christian leaders of the eighteenth century*).

1

A Promising Girlhood

'How many children does Doctor Annesley have?'

'I am not sure, but it is either two dozen or a quarter of a hundred.'[1]

This conversation took place in London in 1669, following the christening of yet another child recently born into the Annesley home. And the latter estimate proved correct; this was indeed the twenty-fifth child to take its place in the doctor's family.

The future of this infant was far from ordinary. This little one, a girl, was to have a very important part in the history of the church. Given the name Susanna, she would grow up to marry Samuel Wesley and to bear nineteen children of her own. Two of her sons would rise to great prominence in the founding of Methodism and would leave mankind good reason to know their accomplishments and to remember their names, both in the field of evangelism and in the writing of hymns, for they were none other than John and Charles Wesley.

Susanna manifestly inherited many of the qualities possessed by her father — beside the tendency to produce a large family. The Reverend Samuel Annesley, M.A., LL.D., was a man of noteworthy character. Born of devout Puritan parents, he stated that he was so early instructed in the way of salvation that he could not remember a time when he was conscious of not knowing the Lord. At the age of five he began to read twenty chapters of the Bible a day and this practice he continued till the close of his life. Early in his teens he entered Oxford University and upon graduating in 1644 he was ordained and became the pastor of a church in the county of Kent.

His actions soon demonstrated what kind of man he was. The previous pastor had joined with his people in their 'dancing, drinking and merriment on the Lord's day'. But Samuel Annesley declared his opposition to all such worldly behaviour and 'they hailed him with spits, forks and stones' and threatened his life. His reply was, 'Use me as you will, I am resolved to continue with you till God has fitted you, by my ministry, to entertain a better man.'[2] He stayed with them till there was evidence of a widespread turning to better practices, when he moved to London.

There he faced still greater difficulties. During the 1640s England had endured a civil war, with, on the one hand, the Royalist army fighting for the king and the Church of England, and on the other, the army of the Parliamentarians, demanding a Puritan form of government. The Parliamentarians, under Oliver Cromwell, were victorious and the king, Charles I, was captured, tried and beheaded. A form of peace was then established, but could not destroy the bitter hostility in men's hearts throughout the nation.

After a few years the Royalists regained power and King Charles II acceded to the throne. In 1662, in the hope of stamping out all traces of Puritanism, Parliament passed the Act of Uniformity. It commanded all ministers to conform to the beliefs and practices of the Church of England. Some 2,000 refused to submit to this edict and, in what became known as the Great Ejection, these men, called nonconformists or Dissenters, were driven out from their positions in the universities, from their churches and from their parsonages. They were forbidden to preach, and were turned out with their wives and families, often to face homelessness and utter poverty. The authorities kept a strict watch on their activities and the slightest attempt to hold a religious service could bring a man a heavy fine, or several years in a foul jail, or banishment to semi-slavery in a foreign land. It was as a result of this law that John Bunyan suffered his now celebrated imprisonment.

Samuel Annesley was one of these 2,000 brave men. His action cost him a salary of £700 a year, and although he appears to have found other employment, his family undoubtedly suffered some loss and deprivation. His activities were constantly watched by the Royalist officials, and although he was never arrested there was an occasion on which an officer suddenly fell to the floor, dead, in the very act of signing a warrant for his arrest. But the danger of being seized and thrown into prison was always hanging over him and must have been a constant strain on his wife and family as well as himself.

Susanna's mother also appears to have been a person of great strength of character. Samuel Annesley's first wife had died at the birth of their first child. He remarried and this second wife bore the other twenty-four children, several of whom died in infancy. It is said of her that 'The few dim intimations concerning her impress us with the idea that she was a woman of superior understanding and earnest and constant purity. She spared no labour in endeavouring to promote the religious welfare of her numerous children.'[3] She must also have been hard-working and endowed with remarkable patience, to have borne and brought up so large a family.

After the Dissenters had endured the prohibition on their worship for ten years, the king, Charles II, relaxed some of the laws forbidding their activity. The majority of the ejected men who were still alive immediately launched into vigorous ministries.

Dr Annesley was particularly aggressive. Leasing a meeting-house in a London district known as Little St Helen's, Bishopsgate Street, he soon built up a flourishing congregation. He loved his flock and was loved by them, and from the subjects dealt with in his preaching he appears to have fed them on the meat as well as the milk of the Word of God. It is said of him: 'He lived in the unclouded light of the divine countenance';[4] 'Many called him the instrument of their conversion'; and 'During the next quarter of a century he was one of the most attractive, laborious and useful preachers of his day.' The forces of nonconformity looked upon him as their most prominent figure and their leader.

Samuel Annesley also became known for his generosity. He gave liberally to widows and orphans, the sick and afflicted regarded him as their friend and the needy flocked to his house. Both in the pulpit and out of it, he was a striking personality, and a biographer has stated, 'His personal appearance was noble and commanding. "Fine figure," "dignified mien", "highly expressive and amiable countenance" are the phrases used by his contemporaries. Hardy in constitution and almost insensible to cold, hat, gloves and top-coat were no necessities to him, even in the depths of winter. The days of hoar frost and chilling winds found him in his study at the top of his house, with open window and empty fire-grate. Temperate in all things, he needed no stimulants, and from his infancy hardly ever drank anything but water. He could endure any amount of toil, preaching twice or thrice every day of the week without any sense of weariness. Until the time when the divine voice said unto him, "Get thee up and die," his "eye was not dim nor his natural force abated".[5]

It is evident that from such a father Susanna would have inherited gifts of a rich and unusual nature, and these qualities would have been complemented by those which she received from her capable mother.

During the years of his pastorate in Little Saint Helen's, Samuel Annesley lived in Spital Yard, a street of good homes in a highly respectable district. And in this house his children grew up. The names of all the twenty-five have not been recorded. But we know those of two of the boys: Samuel and Benjamin. And as to the girls, we know of five; Judith, Anne, Elizabeth and Sarah, and, of course, the youngest of the family, Susanna.

We have reason to believe that these children grew up in a peaceful home. We may be sure that even during the period when he was harassed by the authorities Dr Annesley steadily maintained his self-control and that although he demanded obedience from his youngsters he never gave way to outbursts of temper. And after the law against Dissenters was relaxed, the atmosphere in the Annesley home would undoubtedly have been even more one of peace and concord.

This was the background in which Susanna grew up. We can only wish that more information was available about her early years, that reports existed of her as a little girl, playing with her sisters, learning to read, acquiring knowledge and growing into her teenage years. But of these things we are told very little.

However, she speaks of 'preservation from ill accidents and once from a violent death'.[6] Since in those days large open fireplaces were used for heating, and lighting was by candles, fires were frequent occurrences and she may well be referring to an escape from fire at some point in her childhood. And since horses and boats were the common means of travel it is likely that she may have come near to losing her life in an accident involving one or other of these.

The question arises, 'What education did Susanna have?' She may have attended a local grammar school, or have been taught at home by her father or by one of her older sisters, and it is possible that she was instructed by a private tutor. Certain authors have assumed that she came to be versed in French, Latin and Greek, but this was not the case. Nevertheless, throughout her days as a busy mother and as the teacher of her own children, she revealed a fully trained and richly stored mind. She used the English language with precision and possessed a theological knowledge superior to that of many ministers of that day, or this. Her life was governed by a self-discipline that allowed not the least deviation from its principle and purpose. The universities did not admit women in those days, but if they had done so, we may be sure that she would have proved as able a scholar as any of her three sons.

And what about Susanna's religious practices as a young girl? Many years later, in a letter to her son John, she stated, 'I will tell you what rule I observed ... when I was young, and too much addicted to childish diversions, which was this — never to spend more time in mere recreation in one day than I spent in private religious devotions.'[7] Here was the principle of her life put into practice. She also tells of making much use of 'good books'. She was the kind of person who would never give a second thought to even the best of the literature that had been produced by the Restoration authors, but with her father's library available she undoubtedly read certain of the Reformers and the Puritans, difficult as their works would seem for a young girl to read.

Was Susanna converted while she was still a girl? Certainly two years before she died she had an experience which her sons Charles and John regarded as her conversion, declaring that until that event she was in 'a legal night'. However, several persons have objected to that description of her, asserting that she had displayed the marks of true Christianity ever since her childhood. But as we examine her life in the coming chapters we shall see evidence of a confusion in her mind as to how one becomes a Christian, as, on the one hand, she frequently declared the need of faith and of a belief in the heart, but also manifested at times a reliance on human works. Whatever her true state at this time, we can rejoice that she ultimately came into a full assurance of salvation through the experience that her sons considered to be her conversion.

During Susanna's childhood, the Annesley home was visited by several of her father's associates, leaders of the Dissenting cause. Among these men were some of the most learned ministers of the century, including, for example, Thomas Manton, whose *Works* occupy twenty-two volumes, and Richard Baxter, the author of numerous books, of which the best-remembered are *The Reformed*

Pastor, The Saint's Everlasting Rest and *A Call to the Unconverted*. But the most eminent of all those who came was John Owen, formerly Vice-Chancellor of Oxford University, famous as a theologian and esteemed as the 'Prince of Puritans' and many of whose books are still in print and highly prized in our own day.

These men and others who visited the Annesley home talked frequently of the subject uppermost in their minds: the differences between the Church of England and themselves. This meant that from her earliest days, Susanna listened to this matter being discussed by exceptionally capable men, and heard every argument against the church and in favour of Dissent presented with logic and force. She also knew that her father had endured ejection from his church and had suffered the loss of a considerable salary because of his convictions in the Dissenting cause, and it would not have been strange had she manifested a distinct hostility towards the Church of England, its people and all of its clergy.

But the opposite proved to be the case. Despite having heard so much to persuade her to the contrary, Susanna gradually came to the conclusion that Dissent was wrong and the Church of England was right. She wrote out a report of her reasoning in the matter, but it was burned in the fire that later destroyed the Epworth rectory. She tells us, however, 'Because I had been educated among the Dissenters, and there being something remarkable in my leaving them at so early an age, not being full thirteen, I had drawn up an account of the whole transaction, under which I included the main of the controversy between them and the Established Church, as far as it had come to my knowledge.'[8]

It would be very interesting to know all that she included in this account. She says she dealt with 'the main of the controversy', which indicates that she must have considered the historical events of the conflict and the arguments in favour of the hierarchy of the church, as opposed to the unorganized condition of the Dissenters. Nowhere does she give any indication that she sought to discover the doctrine of the church taught in the New Testament, but she evidently assumed she must choose between these two systems, and she turned to the one she felt was the better of the two.

Having made this decision, Susanna quitted the church of which her father was pastor and was received into one belonging to the Church of England. Samuel Annesley had sacrificed and suffered for the cause of Dissent and he could not have failed to be sorely aggrieved by this action on the part of his youngest daughter. There is much reason to believe that Susanna's relationship with her parents was, to say the least, strained from this point onwards. We notice, too, how young she was. She was, in her own words, 'not full thirteen'. Here was a girl displaying an independence of mind and a strength of decision virtually unheard of in a child so young. Here was a girl who gave promise of living a rich life and of growing into a woman of remarkable force of character. And if, as was especially true in those times, a woman's greatest accomplishment lay in the qualities she imparted to her offspring, then her chief achievement would be witnessed, not in her successful teaching of her children, nor in the exercise of her unbounded patience, but rather, as we shall see, in the transmission to her sons, by natural inheritance, of her independence of mind, her strength of decision and her numerous other rare qualities.

Samuel Wesley admits that he was too keen and revengeful, and that if he thought a person had injured him, he could not forgive such a person without receiving something he thought was a satisfaction.

(Luke Tyerman, *The life and times of the Rev. Samuel Wesley, M.A.*).

2

Susanna Annesley Marries Samuel Wesley

The visitors to the Annesley home included others besides mature scholars. Several students came too, and they were drawn not only by the Doctor's experience and knowledge, but also by the presence of his talented and attractive daughters.

One who came was a youth named Daniel Defoe, who was later to achieve prominence as a writer and who is best remembered as the author of *Robinson Crusoe*. Another was John Dunton, who became a noted publisher. He says, concerning the first time he entered Little Saint Helen's Church, 'Instead of engaging my attention to what the Doctor said, I suffered my mind and my eyes to run at random. I soon singled out a young lady who almost charmed me mad.'[1] This was one of the Annesley girls, but to Dunton's immense displeasure she proved to be already engaged. But he quickly took up with her sister Elizabeth and became equally enthralled with her.

Before many months had passed, Dunton and Elizabeth were married. And there at the wedding was Dunton's close friend, a student named Samuel Wesley. As a wedding gift Wesley read before the assembled guests a tribute to the bride and groom that he termed 'an epithalamium'. It was a romantic poem that he had composed and was liberally sprinkled with such expressions as 'little Cupids', 'golden Hymen', 'marble-hearted virgins', 'envious swains' and, of course, 'the charming bride'.

The wedding may well have been the occasion of the first meeting between Susanna and Samuel. He was nineteen at the time but she, although extraordinarily mature for her age, was apparently still no more than thirteen. There is reason to believe that a firm friendship sprang up between them at about this time. It is particularly significant that, just as Susanna had left the Dissenters and had joined the Church of England, so Samuel also now prepared to take the same step.

Like Susanna, Samuel had grown up under the teachings of Dissent. Four months before he was born, his father had been a victim of the Great Ejection. Refusing to conform to the practices of the Church of England, he was turned out of his church and his parsonage and was forbidden to preach. With his pregnant wife he fled to another town in his native Dorsetshire, only to find that he was refused entry. He moved on to one town after another, and he defied the authorities by preaching virtually every day. As the months went by he was arrested three times, served the sentence each time and was released, but during a fourth incarceration, in which he was forced to sleep on the cold, bare earth of the loathsome prison, he fell ill and soon died. He was only forty-two, a martyr for the Dissenting cause.

While Samuel's father suffered greatly, all this was especially hard for his mother. She had come from an excellent family, for her father had been a member of the committee that produced the *Westminster Confession of Faith*, and she was also a niece of the eminent historian, Dr Thomas Fuller. Yet after only a few years of married life, this worthy woman suffered this long period of homelessness, to which was added the pain of losing her husband. Very little is known about her life at the time, but twenty years later we find her living in poverty in London and maintained by the kindness of her sons.

Samuel was cared for during his schoolboy years by friends among the Dissenters, some of whom, recognizing special qualities in him and believing that he intended to enter the Dissenting ministry, were responsible for his being placed at the age of fifteen in one of their academies in London. Although men who were not members of the Church of England could enter the universities, they were not allowed to graduate and therefore the Dissenters had established these institutions, most of which maintained an academic standard as high as that of Oxford or Cambridge.

During his time at the Dissenting academy, Samuel proved himself a capable student and became learned in classical studies. But he was also impulsive and quick-tempered and he confesses that he 'had a narrow escape from debauchery and ruin'.[2]

After spending four years in the academy, young Wesley was

planning to attend Oxford University. He tells us that Dr Owen was sure that times were soon to change, and the Dissenters would be allowed to graduate from the universities, and he counselled Samuel to attend in the expectation that he would be able to graduate when the change in the ruling came about.[3]

Samuel, however, was not merely thinking of following Dr Owen's plan; he was considering going all the way — leaving the Dissenters and joining the Church of England. He claims that he had witnessed certain actions among Dissenting men that made him loth to remain in fellowship with them. His whole outlook on life also leads us to believe that he saw greater possibilities of advancement within the hierarchical system of the Church of England than in the lack of organization that characterized the Dissenting cause.

There is good reason to believe that Samuel would have discussed this matter of church versus Dissent with Susanna, who had recently been through a similar experience, and who would still have clear in her mind the reasoning which had caused her to take so serious a step. Although there is no document actually reporting such conversations, we may be sure that they took place. We do know that, as part of his work at the academy, Samuel was asked to research all the reasons in favour of Dissent, and he says, 'I found I lived in groundless separation from the Established Church.'[4]

Accordingly, in characteristic manner, he quickly took action. Notwithstanding the great moral debt he owed to Dissent, he left the church of which he had been a member and joined one belonging to the Church of England. Now he would go to Oxford, not as an outsider who had merely been allowed to attend, but as a fully fledged member of the university. Moreover, when he had obtained his degree he would seek ordination in the Church of England and would spend the rest of his life in the ministry of that church.

However, supporting himself throughout a five-year course was a weighty undertaking for a fatherless youth, the son of a penniless mother. In fact, Samuel had already incurred debts, but he accepted a grant of £30 from a Dissenting fund[5] and paid what he owed. Then, since he lived with his mother and knew his action would severely distress her, he said nothing about his intentions. Instead, he got up very early one morning and, carrying his earthly possessions in a bag slung over his shoulder, he 'footed it' to Oxford, where he entered himself as a servitor at Exeter College. The date was August 1683.

In this capacity Samuel had to wait upon one or two students who were financially better off. These duties freed him from paying for his tuition, but he was still responsible for the cost of his books, his food and his clothing, and during the winter months for the fuel he burned in his fireplace. Samuel launched himself into the task of obtaining money, doing so with his usual fervour and determination.

First, he wrote to relatives and visited acquaintances seeking help, 'till they grew weary,' he says, 'of my asking and I of doing so.'[6] But these requests brought him nothing.

Secondly, he published in booklet form some poems he had written. He possessed a definite gift for writing verse and he now brought out into the open certain items he had composed during his schooldays. The booklet, which he entitled *Maggots*, contained verse with such titles as 'A snake in a box of bran', 'The grunting of a hog', 'To my gingerbread mistress', 'The bear-faced lady', 'A pair of breeches', 'A cow's tail' and 'A box like an egg'. This work did bring him some income but the titles attracted the ridicule of his fellow-students.

Even so, Samuel's poverty did not prevent him from coming to the aid of a child in still greater need than himself. His first winter in Oxford was one of the coldest on record and as he was walking one morning, he came upon a small boy, very poorly clad, lying beneath a hedge and crying from hunger and cold. Samuel had in his pocket two pennies — all that he owned — but he was so moved by the little lad's suffering that he gave him both of them. The boy ran to buy bread for himself and his still younger sister.[7] But a very welcome surprise greeted the now penniless Samuel when he returned to his college. He found that a relative had sent him five shillings and that a gift from his mother was waiting for him. She had sent him a cheese.

As the months went by, while Samuel was proving himself to be a diligent and capable student, there came an occasion on which he found himself unable to pay his battels — his accounts for provisions from the college kitchen. He was pressed for payment and, since he could see no means of obtaining money, he faced the sad prospect of having to leave the university and seeing all his efforts to put himself through five years of study ending in failure. In preparation for his departure he wrote a poem bidding a sorrowful farewell to Oxford. But when returning a book he had borrowed he accidentally left this poem in it. The owner of the book, a senior student, found these farewell verses and was so moved by them that

Samuel Wesley

he took steps to see that Wesley would not need to leave the university. First, he paid Wesley's battels himself and then he arranged for certain students who needed help in their studies to use Samuel as their tutor.[8] He also got them to agree to pay him exceptionally well for his services.

Samuel was well able to undertake these added duties while he continued with his own academic work. Moreover, the remuneration was so high that his circumstances now took on a totally new complexion. This extra work proved available as long as he remained at the university, so that he could say, 'I continued in plenty and prosperity till ready for my degree.' He also did some important translation work for the Bodleian Library, and this added still further to his income.

Finally, after five years in Oxford, there arrived the occasion that Samuel had been anticipating. In June 1688 he graduated,[9] and was awarded the degree of Bachelor of Arts of Oxford University. He deserves much credit for his determination and his scholastic ability, but recognition is also due to the man who paid his battels for him and arranged for the other students to pay him so well for his tutoring.

Immediately after graduating Samuel returned to London. Within a short space of time he was ordained as a minister of the Church of England and secured a curacy that paid him £28 a year. And now that he had a regular income his first thought was about marrying the girl he had known for six years, Susanna Annesley.

There is no record of any letters between them during his days in Oxford, but the circumstances require us to believe that they must have written to each other. At any rate, the association was now renewed and without any time-consuming effort on his part, or any feminine refusals on hers, they arranged to be married.

The ceremony took place on 11 November 1688.[10] Where it was performed is not known, but we may be certain that it was a Church of England service. Susanna's father would not have been allowed to take any part in conducting the rite, but it is to be hoped that he and his family were at least present to witness the marriage.

No description has come down to us of Susanna's physical appearance at this time, but we do have one of her sister, which reads: 'She is tall; of good aspect; her hair of a light chestnut colour; dark eyes, her eye-brows dark and even; her mouth little and sufficiently sweet; her air somewhat melancholy, sweet and agreeable; her neck long and graceful; white hands, a well-shaped body; her complexion very fair.'[11] Sir Peter Lely, a prominent artist of those times, painted a portrait of Susanna's sister Judith, displaying, we are told, 'a very beautiful woman'. But someone who knew them both declared, 'Beautiful as Judith Annesley is, she is far from being as beautiful as Mrs Wesley.'

Susanna and Samuel were alike in that each had left the Dissenting background in which they had been brought up and had become very hearty adherents of the Church of England. But in other ways they were very different. Susanna was much the taller of the two and carried herself in an easy but dignified manner. Samuel was only about five feet four and his bearing had something military and autocratic about it. Thoughts constantly flowed in his mind in the form of meter and rhyme, but while there was rich beauty in her language she possessed nothing of his poetic skill. His speech was frequently marked by wit and humour, but although she revealed a deep inner peace there is no record of her joking or even laughing. She makes no mention of her emotions in being joined to Samuel, but he says of his being married, 'for doing which before my fortunes were settled, I have no excuse, unless a most passionate love may be taken for one'.[12]

At the time of their marriage Samuel was twenty-six and Susanna nineteen. Before them lay the years of their life together as husband and wife, and we now follow that story, with its hills and its valleys, its trials and its triumphs, 'till death did them part'.

Therefore as the church is subject unto Christ, so let the wives be to their own husbands in everything.
Husbands, love your wives, even as Christ also loved the church, and gave himself for it.

(Ephesians 5:24-25).

3

Early Years of Married Life

Samuel stayed merely a few months in his London curacy. Finding it difficult to live on £28 a year, when he was offered an opportunity to acquire, as he said, 'some moneys to begin the world with', he accepted it. This was the position of chaplain aboard a naval vessel on the Irish Sea and it promised him £70 per annum.

But he did not remain here long either. 'I was very ill used,' he reported, 'and almost starved and poisoned, the captain for a great part of the time keeping no table, nor had we either fish, or butter, or cheese in the ship, and our beef stunk intolerably.'[1] He left after six months and was then told he must wait to receive his wages. He returned to London, virtually unemployed. During his absence Susanna had lived in a boarding-house and he joined her there.

However, Susanna was now pregnant, and as the time of her delivery approached she returned to her parents' home.[2] We must assume that despite any coolness that had existed between her father and herself, her family realized that she needed a better place than a boarding-house in which to give birth to her first child. Accordingly, on 10 February 1690, in the home in which she had spent her girlhood, she gave birth to a son, who, like his father and grandfather, was given the name of Samuel.

It would seem that the birth was a difficult one and a trying experience for Susanna, even though there probably was a capable midwife to attend her. Years later, in a letter written to this son when he had grown up, she was to address him in the words: 'you, my son — you who was once the son of my extremest sorrow in your birth...'

Samuel Wesley next gained employment as a curate in the

suburb of Newington Butts, but he divided his time between his clerical duties and some literary work in London, and this displeased the rector of the church, who told him he was no longer wanted. Samuel and Susanna returned to the boarding-house, where Samuel continued his literary labours. But the income he received from these was small and he speaks of himself as being very downhearted. He longed, he says, 'for a place of peace and quiet' where he could write without obstruction. And just such a place he was now offered. He tells of visiting a home in the suburb of Hackney where he met a Colonel Mildmay. The colonel told him that he had a living to dispose of, the rectorship of St Leonard's Church, in South Ormsby, Lincolnshire.[3] This offer Samuel immediately accepted.

Samuel already owed a sum of money to the owner of the boarding-house, and the cost of transporting himself and his family to his new parish increased his debt. He says, 'I met with no inconsiderable difficulties in getting thither, lying sometimes money-bound here in town, being also indebted for my wife's board and my own... I could not have stirred had not my patroness graciously offered to furnish me with what money I wanted on my note to repay it. Accordingly, I had £10 of her when I set out with my family, and ten more when I came to housekeeping.'[4]

As we read the story before us, we shall see Samuel in debt throughout his life, right up to the time of his death. However much our hearts are stirred by compassion, it is difficult, when we note the readiness with which he accepted these loans from his anonymous patroness, not to feel that he was inclined to rush too easily into debt.

His debt increased still further when he reached South Ormsby. He possessed no furniture and, having it all now to buy, he expected that Dr Annesley would provide the money, 'which,' he remarks, 'he did not one quarter perform'. Apparently the Dissenting doctor was not ready to assist his Anglican son-in-law by furnishing his house for him!

Samuel began his duties in South Ormsby in June 1690. The population of the village was about 260 and he was to receive £50 a year. There was a rectory, but it was a poor primitive place, 'composed of reeds and clay'.

We do well to remind ourselves that such a house, in a country village, was completely lacking in the host of conveniences that are found in almost all of our houses today. There was no electricity for lighting or heating and none of the domestic appliances that operate

Bed belonging to Samuel and Susanna Wesley, preserved at the Old Rectory, Epworth

Susanna's workbox, preserved at the Old Rectory, Epworth

on it, no refrigerator, radio or television, no telephone or running water. There were fires to light and water had to be drawn from a well or carried from a stream. Because everything had to be done by hand, all but the poorest homes would employ a girl as a servant, and such help could be obtained for about fourpence a day. The Wesleys kept one servant most of the time and on occasions when Susanna was incapacitated they had two. This was not a special privilege, but was the practice in a large number of homes, and would have been expected in a clergyman's household.

Samuel and Susanna settled down to life in South Ormsby. He was the soul of industry and besides performing his clerical duties he laboured at literary undertakings. John Dunton, his brother-in-law in London, produced a bi-weekly journal, the *Athenian Gazette,* and Samuel was a partner in this publication, regularly contributing articles.

Readers were invited to send in their questions and Wesley was responsible for answering them. These enquiries included such topics as, 'On what day did Adam fall?' 'How do angels eat?' 'How shall infants and deformed persons rise at the Day of Judgement?' and 'Whither went the waters of Noah's flood?'[5] The answers Samuel gave to questions like these were undoubtedly more speculative than biblical. However, other questions were in the realms of theology and philosophy, and in answering these Samuel revealed a breadth of knowledge that was rare in a man of his age. He also published during these first months in South Ormsby two books, *An essay upon all sorts of learning,* and *A discourse concerning the antiquity and authority of Hebrew vowel points.* These works not only revealed Samuel's scholarship, but they tended to parade it, and to manifest a measure of self-importance which was to be found in virtually all of his writings.

This latter tendency also characterized Samuel's relationship with Susanna. Of course, in that century it was customary for a man to act as 'king of the castle' in his own home, and his wife was expected to serve him. Samuel's attitude towards Susanna is expressed in some lines that he wrote during these days:

She graced my humble roof, and blest my life,
Blest me by a far greater name than wife;
Yet still I bore an undisputed sway,
Nor was't her task, but pleasure to obey:

Scarce thought, much less could act, what I denied.
In our low house there was no room for pride;
Nor need I e'er direct what still was right,
She studied my convenience day and night.
Nor did I for her care ungrateful prove,
But only used my power to show my love;
Whate'er she asked I gave without reproach or grudge,
For still she reason asked, and I was judge.[6]

This was Samuel's appraisal of his relationship with his wife. She proved a distinct blessing to his life, yet he subjected her to his 'undisputed sway' and her pleasure was to be found in obeying him. As we have seen, before her marriage she had been a girl of strongly independent mind, but now she could scarcely think, 'much less could act', in any manner in which he did not fully acquiesce. He declared his gratitude that she placed his convenience first, and although he gave her whatever she asked, he was ever the judge as to what she should ask.

So we see that married life was not proving a great success from Susanna's point of view. Not only was she not allowed a mind of her own, they were also living in poverty and her husband was constantly in debt. She had grown up in her father's comfortable home, but since marrying Samuel Wesley she had lived, first in the boarding-house, and now in this primitive rectory at South Ormsby. Similarly, her father had never known financial need, but it was becoming obvious that Samuel would probably remain in debt for the rest of his days. So by the time she had been married a few months Susanna must have come to realize that submission and poverty were likely to be permanent features of her life.

Susanna was by now pregnant for the second time. When she and Samuel had been in South Ormsby seven months another child was born. This was a girl and was named, like herself, Susanna.

A year later Susanna was again expecting a child. Samuel displayed an unfeeling attitude towards her, speaking of, '... my wife's lying about last Christmas and threatening to do the same the next, and 2 children and as many servants to provide for (my wife being sickly, having had 3 or 4 touches of her rheumatism again, though we always fight it away with whey)'.[7] This child they called Emilia.

At this time Susanna and Samuel faced a grave disappointment over their first child, Sammy. They had early determined that he should become a clergyman, but to their dismay he failed to begin to speak. By the time he was four they assumed he was a deaf mute and their hopes of seeing him enter the ministry were dashed. One morning, however, Susanna could not find him and she went through the house and out into the yard, looking for him. She was afraid he might have come to some harm, and even though she did not think he could hear, she constantly called his name. Finally she heard a child's voice say, 'Here I am, mamma,' and glancing down she saw Sammy underneath a table, holding his favourite cat in his arms. From that point onwards he talked as normally as any other child.

After he had been rector of South Ormsby for four years Wesley's name was put forward as a candidate for a much higher position in the church. In a mansion adjacent to the village there lived a member of the aristocracy, the Marquis of Normanby. Some time earlier the marquis had made Wesley his domestic chaplain and he now wrote to Dr Tillotson, the Archbishop of Canterbury, suggesting that he appoint Wesley to a vacant bishopric in Ireland. Of course, Wesley, who was still only in his early thirties, lacked the maturity and experience necessary for such a responsibility, and the request was refused.[8] A short time later two of Wesley's long-time associates, John Dunton and Daniel Defoe, claimed that he had himself asked the marquis to suggest him for the post and their assertion is undoubtedly true.

Nothing daunted, Samuel continued his search for advancement. In 1688 England had experienced a revolution in which the Catholic King James had been exiled, and his daughter Mary and her husband, William of Orange, had acceded to the throne. But William, a member of the royal family of Holland, had no true heritage in England, and although he was a strong Protestant, many people refused to swear allegiance to him. Mary, who had a right to the throne, was accepted by the majority, but she still sought declarations of loyalty from her subjects.

Such a need Samuel Wesley now supplied. He requested, and received, permission to dedicate to the queen a book he had recently written entitled, *The life of our blessed Lord and Saviour Jesus Christ, a heroic poem.* It was prefaced with 'A discourse concerning heroic poetry,' and was illustrated with sixty copper plates. How much of it the queen actually read is not known, but at least it brought Samuel Wesley to her attention, displayed his poetic taste and declared his loyalty to her and to King William. It also addressed the queen in highly flattering terms. To gain the good will of the sovereign was an exceptionally valuable step, for she had at her command numerous ecclesiastical privileges and positions, and Wesley said that because of this book she appointed him to his next charge, which was, as we shall see, the parish of Epworth.

Samuel now took two other steps with a view to improving his position. Firstly, he received the degree of Master of Arts from Cambridge University, and secondly, he gained the curacy of another place which he says was 'a mile or two from my own'. This was the parish of South Thoresby, and two years later he also acquired the parish of Swaby. He reports that the additions 'added to my fortunes', and although the amounts involved were probably small, the assumption of the responsibility for these churches indicates Samuel's industry and his determination to succeed.

It was at this time, in 1694, that the Wesleys first witnessed the entrance of death into their home. Their second child, Susanna, had been sickly for some months; she grew steadily worse and finally passed away. It must have been especially painful for the mother to have to watch this little one gradually weaken, in spite of all that was done for her, till her life was taken. Susanna was to face this grim experience over and over again, for nine of her children. Much of her adult life was taken up with bearing children and watching them die.

In fact, she was to lose two more children very shortly after this first death. Early in 1695 Susanna gave birth to twin boys, who lived for only a month. She had not had time fully to regain her strength after the double births before she had the sorrow of seeing these two little ones placed in their graves.

Not long after this, she learned that her father was unwell. Dr Annesley had enjoyed vibrant health for most of his life, but in 1696 he became ill. The cost of travel, as well as family duties, would prohibit Susanna from visiting him in London, and besides praying for him all she could do was to wait for letters reporting his condition.

We are told that, as Dr Annesley lay suffering, 'His mind had so long been filled with thoughts of God that even in moments of mental wandering he still breathed the same spirit... Then the floods of holy joy so inundated his soul that he exclaimed, "I cannot contain it! What manner of love is this to a poor worm! I cannot express a thousandth part of what praise is due to thee... I will die praising thee! ... I shall be satisfied with thy likeness! Satisfied! Satisfied! O, my dearest Lord Jesus, I come!'"⁹ At the age of seventy-seven Samuel Annesley went to abide in the joy of the presence of God. There is no record of the amount of Dr Annesley's possessions at the time of his death. One author suggests that he had been earning between £300 and £400 a year and another mentions £700. But his will reads, 'My just debts being paid, I give to each of my children one shilling, and all the rest to be divided between my son Benjamin, my daughter Judith and my daughter Anne.' He may have been unaware of the poverty the Wesleys were suffering, or his failure to include Susanna's name along with her sisters and her brother may have been the result of his displeasure at her having left Dissent for the Church of England. In either case, the absence of any mention of her name from his will must have been a disappointment to her.

None the less, she was sorely moved by his death — so much so that she could hardly bring herself to believe he had truly departed from this earth. In later years, 'Her son John heard her say that she was frequently as fully persuaded that her father was with her as if she had seen him with her bodily eyes.' She firmly believed in the reality of the spirit world and was convinced that she frequently communed with his spirit.

The hope that Samuel Wesley had entertained in flattering Queen Mary in his *Life of Christ* — that she would appoint him to a more prominent parish and one that paid better — now came to fruition in a small measure, when he was appointed rector of the parish of the Lincolnshire town of Epworth. He stated, 'Queen Mary gave me this benefice,' but recent research has shown that he received it as a gift from the king. At least, he was right that a royal hand was behind the favour.

Accordingly, Susanna and Samuel prepared to leave South Ormsby. They had been there for six, or perhaps seven years, and it had proved a place of disappointment and almost constant child-bearing for her, and of literary labour and ever-increasing debt for him. But now they both hoped that brighter skies were before them. This they expected would be true especially in the financial realm, for whereas Samuel's salary at South Ormsby had been a mere £50, he was informed that it would now be virtually £200. So, with this prospect of better times awaiting them, they said their farewells, loaded their waggons and set out for Epworth.

Epworth parish church, where Samuel was rector for thirty-eight years

The association of this town with the Wesley family was to establish its name in loving remembrance the world over for generations to come.

Anger, and some sort of aversion, I own to be more difficult to subdue when we meet with any displeasing object, though even these have too often pride or interest at the bottom; and if we reflect justly, we shall find we are seldom angry but when one of them is touched upon. Either we think our *mighty* selves are affronted, or there is something of rivalship in the case, and another obtains what we think is our due.

(Samuel Wesley, 1706).

4

Forsaken by Her Husband

Although separated by several miles from the ocean, Epworth was actually located on an island. Three rivers converged and enclosed a portion of land some fourteen miles in length, and the encircled area was known as the Isle of Axholme. A large majority of the inhabitants were unlettered and some were vicious, but a few were of a better class. Here, after arriving in 1697, Samuel and Susanna were to remain till his death thirty-eight years later.

Susanna was not one to glory in material things, but we may be sure that, at least for her family's sake, she was pleased to move into a rectory that was larger and somewhat better than the one at South Ormsby. 'It contained five bays, built all of timber and plaster, and covered all with straw thatch, the whole building being contrived into three storeys, and being disposed in seven chief rooms — a kitchen, a hall, a parlour, a buttery and three large upper rooms and some others of common use...' [1] The Wesleys undoubtedly delighted in this improvement in their domestic circumstances.

Having made the step upwards from South Ormsby to Epworth, Samuel had reason to hope that further advancement lay before him. Immediately after his appointment he was asked to go to Gainsborough and preach the Visitation Sermon, and among his hearers were the bishop and a majority of the clergy of the diocese. He was also invited to journey to London and address the annual meeting of the Society for the Reformation of Manners. At this gathering his audience would include not only a number of ministers, but also certain members of the aristocracy—people of wealth and influence. But Samuel had to meet his own expenses in travelling to and from these events.

A still greater honour followed when he was elected to serve as a proctor (that is, a representative) of the diocese of Lincoln at the Convocation of the Church of England. The convocation was held in London and was virtually an ecclesiastical parliament that legislated concerning the affairs of the church. 'The lower house of which Mr Wesley was a member consisted of twenty-two deans, fifty-three archdeacons, twenty-four prebendaries and forty-four proctors — altogether one hundred and forty-three persons.'[2] Election to this body was a privilege and an honour and the fact that Samuel Wesley was chosen indicates the high opinion in which this new man at Epworth was held by the Lincolnshire clergy. Yet for this visit to London, which might require his presence there for several weeks, he was not paid anything at all, and again he met his own expenses, which he says amounted to £50.

Always a man of intense industry, shortly after his arrival in Epworth, Samuel added to his clerical duties the task of farming. There were some acres of glebe lands owned by his parish and he began to cultivate them, in the hope of reducing his burden of debt. He also acquired a few animals — cows, pigs, chickens and ducks. But he had no previous experience of farming and although his efforts were praiseworthy they increased rather than reduced his debts.

Several authors have assumed that Samuel Wesley's salary at Epworth was 'wretchedly small', but when compared with the amounts paid to clergymen in general it was truly generous. We have seen that in his first curacy he received £28 and at South Ormsby £50. We are told that 'There were hundreds of clergymen whose livings were not worth more than £20 a year and thousands whose livings did not exceed £50.' Fifty years later John Wesley paid his lay preachers £15 a year. Samuel's salary when he began at Epworth amounted to £200, and although it declined in later years, it was still, in comparison, a considerable sum.

But by the year 1700 Samuel was so far in debt that he was becoming almost desperate. On 28 December of that year he described his situation in a letter to Dr Sharpe, the Archbishop of York, saying,

> I must own that I [am] ashamed ... to confess that I [am] three hundred pounds in debt, when I have a living of which I have made two hundred pounds per annum, though I could hardly let it now for eight score.

I doubt not one reason of my being sunk so far is my not understanding worldly affairs, and my aversion to law...

'Twill be no great wonder that when I had but fifty pounds per annum for six or seven years together, and nothing to begin the world with, one child at least per annum, and my wife sick for half that time, that I should run one hundred and fifty pounds behindhand...

When I had the rectory of Epworth given me, my Lord of Sarum was so generous as to pass his word to his goldsmith [banker] for one hundred pounds which I borrowed of him. It cost me very little less than fifty pounds of this in my journey to London, and getting into my living, for the Broad Seal, etc.; and with the other fifty pounds I stopped the mouths of my most importunate creditors.

When I removed to Epworth I was forced to take up fifty pounds more, for setting up a little husbandry ... and buying some part of what was necessary towards furnishing my house, which was larger, as well as my family...

The next year my barn fell, which cost me forty pounds in rebuilding ... and having an aged mother who must have gone to prison if I had not assisted her, she cost me upwards of forty pounds, which obliged me to take up another fifty pounds. I have had but three children born since I came hither, about three years since; but another coming, and my wife incapable of any business in my family, as she has been for almost a quarter of a year; yet we have but one maidservant, to retrench all possible expenses...

Fifty pounds interest and principal I have paid my Lord of Sarum's goldsmith. All which together keeps me necessitous, especially since interest money begins to pinch me...

Humbly asking pardon for this tedious trouble,

I am your grace's most obliged and humble servant,

S. Wesley[3]

Dr Sharpe contributed towards meeting Wesley's need and influenced certain titled people to do so too. Samuel wrote, 'I heartily thank God for raising me so great and generous a benefactor as your grace...,' and he later listed seven persons who had given in response to the archbishop's appeal. Their gifts amounted to £185. Susanna was now pregnant again. Nevertheless Samuel went to London to be present at the convocation, the visit costing him, as he says, £50. When he returned he wrote to the archbishop reporting that Susanna had again given birth to twins. His letter reads:

Epworth, May 16, 1701

My Lord,

This comes to bring such news as I presume will not be unwelcome to a person who has so particular a concern for me. Last night my wife brought me a few children. There are but *two* yet, a boy and a girl, and I think they are all at present; we have had four in two years and a day, three of which are living.

Never came anything more like a gift from heaven than what the Countess of Northampton sent by your charitable offices. Wednesday evening my wife and I clubbed and joined stocks, which came to *six shillings* to send for coals. Thursday morning I received the *ten pounds* and at night my wife was delivered. Glory be to God for his unspeakable goodness!

I am your grace's most obliged and humble servant,

S. Wesley.[4]

Samuel probably regarded his remarks about the birth of the twins as humorous, but we may be sure Susanna would not have thought them so.

However, Samuel was in such low spirits at this time that he could barely think normally. His expectations of securing preferment in the church had failed and his debts seemed ever to mount. He was frustrated and was actually becoming desperate. It is evident he felt he must escape from his circumstances, that he must get away from Epworth and from the pressure of his financial worries. And he now found an opportunity to do just that.

John Wesley was not yet born, of course, but he later heard of his father's incredible action and reported it. His timing is slightly incorrect, but here is what he wrote: 'The year before King William died my father observed my mother did not say *Amen* to the prayer for the king. She said she could not, for she did not believe that the Prince of Orange was king. He vowed he would not cohabit with her till she did. He then took horse and rode away, nor did she hear anything of him for a twelvemonth. He then came back and lived with her as before. But I fear his vow was not forgotten before God.'[5]

We must seek to understand this matter of William of Orange and his not being accepted as the King of England. We have already seen that in 1688 England had experienced a revolution. King James II, who although he professed loyalty to the Church of England, strongly favoured the church of Rome, had been exiled and his daughter Mary had become queen. Her husband, William of Orange, a member of the Dutch royal family, was brought from Holland and was declared king. Though William was a militant Protestant, a considerable body of Englishmen refused to swear allegiance to him and these people were known as 'non-jurors'. Several clergymen were expelled from their livings because of their refusal to recognize William of Orange as sovereign.

Various authors, seeking to maintain that Samuel's character was entirely unblemished, have declared that this 'Amen' affair never happened. They have asserted that John got hold of a false tale and assumed it to be true. The Rev. Luke Tyerman, for instance, says, 'The one damaging point, that Samuel Wesley allowed a miserable squabble respecting the rights of King William to make him neglect his wife, and to leave his house, his family and his flock for the space of twelve months, is a thing which, if true, would have been a scandalous, cruel and wicked act.'[6] But the sad fact is that it is manifestly true.

In 1953 certain letters that Susanna wrote in 1702, during this trying ordeal, came to light and were published in the *Manchester Guardian*. Susanna had informed a non-juror, Lady Yarborough, of Samuel's action. She stated, among other things, that he termed his vow not to live with her 'his oath'. The lady, scarcely able to believe Susanna's report, had replied and Susanna wrote to her again. Here is what she wrote:

To the Lady Yarborough.

                                        Saturday night, March 7, 1701-2.

Madam,

   I'm definitely obliged to you for your charming civility to
a person so utterly unworthy of your favours, but oh, madam!
I must tell your ladyship that you have somewhat mistaken
my case. You advise me to continue with my husband, and
God knows how gladly I would do it, but there, there is my
supreme affliction, he will not live with me. 'Tis but a little
while since he one evening observed in our family prayers
that I did not say Amen to his prayer for KW [King William]
as I usually do to all others; upon which he retired to his study,
and calling me to him asked the reason of my not saying
Amen to the prayer. I was a little surprised at the question and
don't know well what I answered, but too well I remember
what followed: he immediately kneeled down and impre-
cated the divine vengeance upon himself and all his posterity
if ever he touched me more or came into a bed with me before
I had begged God's pardon and his for not saying Amen to the
prayer for the king.
   This, madam, is my unhappy case. I've unsuccessfully
represented to him the unlawfulness and unreasonableness of
his oath; that the man in that case has no more power over his
own body than the woman over hers; that since I'm willing
to let him quietly enjoy his opinions, he ought not to deprive
me of my little liberty of conscience. But he has opened his
mouth to the Lord and what help? ... I have no resentment
against my master, so far from it that the very next day I went
with him to the communion, though he that night forsook my
bed, to which he has been a stranger ever since.
   I'm almost ashamed to own what extreme disturbance this
accident has given me, yet I value not the world. I value
neither reputation, friends or anything in comparison of the
single satisfaction of preserving a conscience void of offence
towards God and man; and how I can do that if I mock
Almighty God for what I think is no sin, is past my discerning.
But I am inexpressibly miserable, for I can see no possibility

of reconciling these differences, though I would submit to anything or do anything in the world to oblige him to live in the house with me.

I appeal to your ladyship if my circumstances are not strangely unhappy. I don't think there's any precedent for such a case in the whole world; and may I not say as the prophet, I am the person that has seen affliction. I'm almost afraid I've already complied with him too far, but most humbly beg your ladyship's direction.[7]

Lady Yarborough had taken up Susanna's case with a friend and this man's opinion had confirmed Susanna in the view that her attitude was correct. Susanna then wrote to Lady Yarborough again, saying:

Madam,

The shortness of my time will I hope excuse the brevity of my answer. I'm extremely obliged to your ladyship for your generous concern and pity of my misfortunes, and return my humblest thanks for your letters, which have been a great cordial to me and given me unspeakable satisfaction. I find the gentleman that has seen my letters is of opinion that I ought not to comply any further, but persevere in following the dictates of my own conscience, which I hope is not erroneous...

I've represented as long as I could be heard the sin of the oath and ill consequences of it to my master, but he cannot be convinced he has done ill, nor does the present change in state [the king's death on 8 March] make any alteration in his mind... He is for London at Easter where he designs to try if he can get a chaplain's place in a man of war [a naval vessel].

I'm more easy in the thoughts of parting because I think we are not likely to live happily together. I have six very little children, which though he tells me he will take very good care of, yet if anything should befall him at sea we should be in no very good condition... I've offered since I last writ to your ladyship to put this business to a reference, provided I might choose one referee and my master another, but I fancy he'll never agree to it. He is fearful of my communicating it to any person, which makes me somewhat more confined than usually. But when he is gone I hope I shall be able to wait on your ladyship...

S.W.

...I humbly beg that the gentleman would be careful that the world may know nothing which may reflect on my master, but that the business may be concealed.[8]

Samuel had sworn his boastful oath on or about 1 March 1702. Yet he had not left home immediately, but though refraining from any familiarity with Susanna, had remained there while he decided what to do.

But on 5 April he left for London. Susanna immediately rode the fourteen miles to the home of Lady Yarborough, and while she was there she wrote to a leading non-juror, Suffragan Bishop Hickes. Her letter to him reads:

Revd Sir,

I should not at this time trouble or divert your better thoughts, but you having been already acquainted by the Lady Yarborough with some uneasy circumstances I at present am under, and expressing so generous a pity and compassion for an unfortunate stranger, makes me presume to beg your direction in this particular.

My master will not be persuaded he has no power over the conscience of his wife, and though I believe he's somewhat troubled over his oath, yet cannot be persuaded 'tis not obligatory. He is now for referring the whole to the Archbishop of York and Bishop of Lincoln, and says if I will not be determined by them, he will do anything rather than live with a person that is the declared enemy of his country...

I know very well before such judges I'm sure to be condemned without a fair hearing; nor can I see any reason I have to ask either God Almighty's or his [Samuel's] pardon for acting according to the best knowledge I have of things of that nature. If I thought or could be persuaded I'm in an error I would freely retract it and ask his pardon before the whole world. He accuses me of pride and obstinacy and insists upon my making him satisfaction for the injury he believes I have done him...

S. Wesley

My master is at London, and the extreme difficulty of receiving a letter when he's at home without his knowledge is the reason I would humbly beg the favour of a speedy answer.[9]

On 29 April Bishop Hickes replied to Susanna's letter. He stated:

Good madam,

The pity and compassion I have for you is no more than what any other person who hath common humanity and Christian charity will declare upon hearing your case... I am persuaded if it were represented to the two persons to whom you say Mr Wesley will refer it, that they would pity you and blame his conduct, and tell him that his oath lays no obligation upon him, but that of repentance for the rashness and iniquity of it, the matter thereof being wholly contrary to the prior obligation of his marriage-promise... It was perjury in him to make it, and will be a continuation of perjury for him to persist in the performance of it...

Perhaps it is advisable for you to state the whole case in a letter to the Archbishop of York and desire him to communicate the same to the Bishop of Lincoln, and to beseech them, if they think his oath unlawful to be kept, they would freely tell him their opinion and charge him to loose himself from the bond of sin...

And to your daily prayers I will add my own, that God would convert him and enable him to follow the blessed life of the meek and charitable Jesus, which he has devoutly celebrated in heroic verse, and proposed for his own as well as other men's example... To that Jesus who himself endured the cross and knows how to comfort all those who endure it, I now commit you with many hearty ejaculations, and remain with all Christian compassion, madam,

Your most faithful friend and servant,

George Hickes[10]

On 31 July Susanna again wrote to Bishop Hickes. She began by referring to receiving his letter and says,

... My master was then at London and had given me time to consider what to do, whether I would submit to his judgement and implicitly obey him in matters of conscience. I foresaw a great many evils would inevitably befall me if I refused to satisfy his desires, and had scarce courage enough to support me in the melancholy prospect when your letter came, which was the noblest cordial and gave me the greatest satisfaction of anything in my whole life.

When he returned he absolutely refused a reference... He stayed two days and then left me early one morning with a resolution never to see me more. But the infinite Power that disposes and overrules the minds of men as he pleases ... so ordered it that in his way he met a clergyman to whom he communicated his intentions, and the reason that induced him to leave his family: he extremely pitied him and condemned me, but, however, he prevailed with him to return.

But as often happens ... his long absenting himself upon that account occasioned abundance of trouble to himself and his family ... as strange a complication of misfortunes as perhaps ever happened to any persons in the world...

Before I've finished my letter I'm alarmed by a new misfortune: my house is now fired by one of my servants, I think not carelessly but by so odd an accident as I may say of it, as the magicians [said] of Moses's fourth miracle, this is the finger of God. Two thirds are burnt, and most of our goods ... are utterly spoiled. May heaven avert all evil from my children and grant that the heavy curse my master has wished upon himself and family may terminate in this life. I most earnestly beg the continuance of your prayers, that God may at last have mercy upon us, at least that he would spare the innocent children, however he is pleased to deal with the unhappy parents.

I am sir

Your most obliged humble servant

S. Wesley.[11]

Of course this was not the fire from which John was rescued; that occurred seven years later. The danger to herself and the children was greater than Susanna states. She herself, though far from well, had taken a child under each arm and had run through the fire and the smoke and reached safety. But in the hurry one of the little girls was left; her cries were heard and some of the neighbours entered the burning building and brought her out through the fire.

Samuel had told his wife that he would never see her again and had set out for London, and by the time the fire was noticed he had got as far as the lower end of the town. When he was told that it was his house that was on fire he must have wondered if the curse that he had pronounced on Susanna and the children was taking effect. Both he and Susanna, like the majority of the people of those times, believed in the power of such curses, and Susanna's prayer that the curse might 'terminate in this life' indicates her apprehensions that its effects could continue even after death. On hearing of the fire, Samuel borrowed a horse and hurried home, where he learned, he says, 'that my wife, children and books were saved'.

There is a question in this affair that needs to be answered. Samuel and Susanna had been married for twelve years when this episode took place and he must have noticed long before this that she did not say 'Amen' to the prayer for the king, which he prayed every day. Why, then, did he wait so long to make his complaint? The reason is undoubtedly that he had willingly allowed her to have her opinion for all those years, but now he had come to such a plight that he must find some excuse for deserting her, and he found it in this matter which he could make appear so tremendously important.

Susanna's refusal to acknowledge William as king manifestly was particularly significant to Samuel as it seemed to place in jeopardy his hopes of securing preferment from the king. He had gained the good will of Queen Mary, but she was now dead. Recently he had produced a memorial of the queen in which he had flattered her in exaggerated terms and he hoped that this would secure the gratitude of the king. But all these hopes would be dashed if it became known that his wife refused to say 'Amen' to the prayer for the sovereign and refused to swear allegiance to him.

Samuel could claim that he had kept his oath. He had left Susanna as he had said he would and had been gone for more than five months. The position he had sought aboard a naval vessel was probably awaiting him. But now that the fire had destroyed a considerable portion of the house he decided to stay at home and rebuild it, using the fire as his justification for doing so.

He wrote at this time to Archbishop Sharpe. He made no reference to his having left Susanna and apparently assumed that the archbishop knew nothing about what he had done. But he did mention the downcast state of mind he had been suffering for some months. 'I find it some happiness,' he said, 'to have been miserable, for my mind has been so blunted with former misfortunes that this [the fire] scarce made any impression on me.'[12]

Samuel's desperate action had two detrimental effects on the life of the Wesleys. For one thing, it hindered Samuel from rising to a better position in the church. He was never appointed to any superior parish and one of the main reasons for his being passed over was no doubt the irresponsibility he had displayed in this affair. And secondly, Susanna's attitude towards him was never the same again, for since he had once shown himself to be so heartless she feared he might well do the same again.

At least this fire had one very valuable result. Had it not occurred and had Samuel spent the remainder of his days aboard a naval vessel, John and Charles would never have been born and the name of Wesley would have been entirely unknown today.

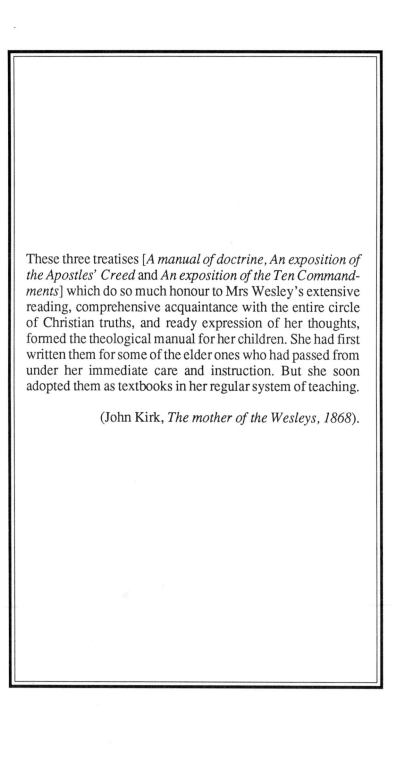

These three treatises [*A manual of doctrine, An exposition of the Apostles' Creed* and *An exposition of the Ten Commandments*] which do so much honour to Mrs Wesley's extensive reading, comprehensive acquaintance with the entire circle of Christian truths, and ready expression of her thoughts, formed the theological manual for her children. She had first written them for some of the elder ones who had passed from under her immediate care and instruction. But she soon adopted them as textbooks in her regular system of teaching.

(John Kirk, *The mother of the Wesleys, 1868*).

5

Susanna's Christian School

When Samuel returned from his five months' absence the relationship between him and Susanna remained one of partial estrangement. From this point onwards Susanna's life was distinctly different from what it had been previously. Her existence now became almost cloistered; she seldom left her house and she devoted all her time and strength to her children. She later explained her chief purpose in doing so and how she concentrated all her efforts to achieve it, saying, 'I have lived such a retired life for so many years... No one can, without renouncing the world in the most literal sense, observe my method; and there are few, if any, that would entirely devote above twenty years of the prime of life in hopes to save the souls of their children.'[1]

In fulfilment of this design Susanna set up a school in her own home. The rebuilding work after the fire was probably not yet completed when she started, but she set apart a room for this purpose and, though she probably did not have proper desks, she apparently found table space for each child. Classes were conducted six days a week, from nine to twelve and then from two till five. 'There was no such thing as loud talking or playing allowed,' stated Susanna, 'but everyone was kept close to business for the six hours of school.'

The Wesley children had, however, been prepared for the control exercised in a school. They had been disciplined since birth. Susanna reported that 'The children were always put into a regular method of living, in such things as they were capable of, from their birth; as in dressing and undressing, changing their linen, etc... When turned a year old (and some before) they were taught to fear the rod and to cry softly, by which means they escaped abundance of correction ... and that most odious noise of the crying of children was rarely heard in the house...'[2]

Lest Susanna's discipline should sound too harsh, we need to view it in the light of the times in which she lived. Heartlessness was widespread. A person could be thrown into prison for owing a few pounds and might be left in this loathsome and disease-ridden confinement to rot and to die. More than a hundred misdemeanours were punishable with death and public hangings were conducted in London with painful frequency. A youth might be seized by a press-gang and forced to labour aboard a ship, where for an unwitting mistake he could be tied to the mast and flogged without mercy. In the schools beating with the birch rod was considered to be as necessary as teaching the alphabet and many parents assumed that physical punishment of their children was as essential for them as eating. In contrast with such conditions Susanna's discipline was light and constructive.

We also need to look at precisely what she says in the paragraph just quoted. We notice the phrase, '... as they were capable of,' and this principle of not pushing a child beyond its natural ability controlled her actions. She says, 'They were taught to fear the rod,' but that does not mean that she used it constantly, or even frequently. They came to realize at an early age that wilful disobedience would result in physical punishment and therefore they learnt to obey. Nor does she say, as some have assumed, that her children were never allowed to cry. Rather her meaning is that when they did cry they did not do so at the top of their lungs. They were not made to repress their emotions totally, but to learn to control the expression of their feelings.

The discipline which Susanna practised from their earliest days was continued as they began to grow. She tells us, 'As soon as they were grown pretty strong they were confined to three meals a day. At dinner their little table and chairs was set by ours, where they could be overlooked; and they were suffered to eat and drink (small beer) as much as they would, but not to call for anything. If they wanted ought they used to whisper to the maid who came and spoke to me; and as soon as they could handle a knife and fork they were set to our table. They were never suffered to choose their meat [food] but always made to eat such things as were provided for the family... Nor were they suffered to go into the kitchen to ask

Part of Susanna's kitchen at the Old Rectory, Epworth, with some of the original utensils

anything of the servants when they were at meat; if it was known that they did so they were certainly beat, and the servants severely reprimanded.'³

The picture painted by Susanna is not one of children living in fear that at any moment a heavy hand might fall upon them, as some have supposed, but rather one of a disciplined household and of children who were conscious that they must obey and generally willing to do so.

Once again Susanna has mentioned her servants. Many women reading her account today may be tempted to think that she did not, after all, have so difficult a life as has been made to appear in these pages, since she had servants. But we need to remember that in those days everything had to be done by hand, that a servant could be obtained for very little more than the cost of her board, and that in view of Mrs Wesley's frequent pregnancies and ill-health it was both normal and necessary for her to have help. Yet she was in no sense living like an aristocrat, having no duties that she needed to perform herself. Rather there were numerous tasks in maintaining the house and the family, over and above those accomplished by the servants; these fell to her and kept all her moments fully occupied.

The strongest criticism levelled against Susanna arises from what she wrote about 'conquering the will' of her children. This is what she said: 'In order to firm the minds of children, the first thing to be done is to conquer their will and bring them to an obedient temper. To inform the understanding is a work of time, and must with children proceed by small degrees as they are able to bear it; but the subjecting the will is a thing that must be done at once, and the sooner the better, for by neglecting timely correction they will contract a stubbornness and obstinacy which are hardly ever after conquered, and never without using such severity as would be as painful to me as to the child... And when the will of a child is totally subdued, and it is brought to revere and stand in awe of the parents, then a great many childish follies and inadvertencies may be passed by. Some should be overlooked and taken no notice of, and others mildly reproved; but no wilful transgression ought ever to be forgiven children without chastisement, less or more, as the nature and circumstances of the offence may require.'⁴

Certainly the idea of conquering the will of a child contradicts much that is taught today about educating children. Yet it is evident that what Susanna meant by this was simply a question of teaching a child that it is under authority and that it is required to obey. It has been suggested that this principle would make children spineless automatons, yet the Wesley children grew up to be men and women who showed great strength of character, one of them to a degree superior to almost all others of his time. Susanna trained her children to obey and in so doing she richly moulded their characters.

As to the degree of learning achieved by the children while still very young, Susanna said that 'It is almost incredible what a child may be taught in a quarter of a year by a vigorous application... All could read better in that time than most women can do as long as they live.'[5] Of course, the Wesley children were quick to learn and their mother was an excellent teacher, but here was extraordinary progress.

Over and above the academic subjects, religious instruction played an important part in this school. Classes opened each morning with the singing of a psalm and the reading of the Scriptures and they closed with the same exercise. The children were trained, as in all avenues of their lives, in decency and politeness, and Susanna said that 'Taking God's name in vain, cursing and swearing, profanity, obscenity, rude ill-bred names, were never heard among them.'[6] They were given a basic knowledge of the Bible and they learned especially to 'remember the sabbath day to keep it holy'.

As we have seen, Susanna had stated that her basic purpose was 'the saving of their souls'. Although her intentions were highly commendable, she failed during these years to mention the substitutionary nature of Christ's death and the receiving of its merits by faith. She said nothing as yet of conversion or of the assurance of salvation, but she stressed the need for regular attendance at church and at the communion, and she seems to have believed that by living a fully disciplined life and refraining from open evil they would be saved.

The intellectual qualities manifested by the Wesley children in their adult life bear witness to the character of the training given by Susanna during their childhood. Each of the three sons possessed, as we shall see and as is widely known, a rich depth of scholarship. And the girls, although denied the educational advantages given to their brothers, possessed, in varying degrees, similarly capable minds. In that day, when even among aristocratic families many women could barely read and write, the Wesley sisters proved truly skilful in their use of the English language and one, Hetty, revealed remarkable ability as a poet.

The strength of character which her children would display in later life was due in part, of course, to inherited qualities, but it also stemmed from their training in Susanna's Christian school.

A noble crop has almost gone, beside Epworth living, to pay some part of those infinite debts my father has run into, that were he to save £50 a year he would not be clear in the world this seven years.

(Emilia Wesley, 1725).

6

Difficulty and Debt

In 1703 an important event in the history of England took place: John Wesley was born.

John largely spent his childhood in female company. His father's hours were devoted to his study and his clerical duties and the home was dominated by the serious but benevolent presence of Susanna. The oldest daughter, Emilia, was now thirteen, Sukey was eight, and they would help to care for their little baby brother. There were also three other sisters: Mary, aged seven, Mehetabel, six and Anne, approaching two. Beside these members of the family there were two maidservants, making a total of eight women and girls whose company John shared during his early boyhood.

When John was only a year old his brother Sammy, who was now fourteen, left home to live in London and attend the celebrated St Peter's School attached to Westminster Abbey. Their father, though little able to bear such expense, was determined to give his boys the best education that the country could provide. Meanwhile the girls and John attended Susanna's school in the rectory.

Susanna did not supply toys for her family. There is a record of their playing cards, but there is no mention of dolls, bats and balls or skipping ropes. None the less, the Wesley children were in no sense joyless. In the evenings they played games, the product of their own imaginations, using whatever materials were at hand. They also made frequent use of books, and since the family was gifted with a rich appreciation of music the sound of children's voices raised in the singing of psalms was often heard during the hours when school was out. There is, however, no evidence of a musical instrument of any kind in the house. They were too poor to afford such an item.

Samuel Wesley's relationship with his children during these years was undoubtedly one of domination on his part, yet it was often also a jovial one. They invariably obeyed him without question, but since he possessed a spontaneous wit he appears to have joked with them when that was his mood.

Samuel was again in debt. We have seen that in 1700 Archbishop Sharpe had raised money towards paying the £300 he owed at that time, and now in 1703 he was again in debt for the same amount. He wrote to Dr Sharpe, thanking him for gifts he had recently received and listing certain of the donors. Among them were a marchioness, a lady, a duke and Queen Anne, all of whom had been influenced by the archbishop to come to his aid.

Despite his need Samuel now became involved in a controversy that caused him to spend still more money. He wrote a letter criticizing the Dissenters' academies and, contrary to his wishes, it was published. Three men, Daniel Defoe, John Dunton and Samuel Palmer, all answered him. Wesley replied to their answer, they responded again and then the whole process was repeated. Wesley pictured himself as the staunch defender of the church and of royalty, but Defoe and Dunton, who had known him since his teenage years, claimed that he praised great people in the hope of gaining preferment. Defoe's biographer also stated that his attack on the Dissenters 'was intended, through royal patronage, to send this time-serving flatterer into the archbishopric of Canterbury...'[1] Even though this statement is obviously exaggerated, we do well to take note of the opinion of Wesley's former companions. This strife did Samuel no good and it proved an additional expense.

Samuel came into further trouble through changing his opinion about candidates in a federal election. Four men were running, two Tories and two Whigs, and at first Wesley declared himself to be in favour of one man from each party. But later, when he learned that the Whigs opposed the church and royalty and that the Tories stood for them, he changed his position and boldly made it known. The election was being fought with anger and even with violence and on the steps of his church Samuel was denounced as a 'rascal and scoundrel'.

His opponents were bitterly hostile and he wrote once more to Archbishop Sharpe, telling him of his difficulties arising from the election, mentioning other troubles and saying,

Epworth, June 7th, 1705

I went to Lincoln on Tuesday night, May 29th, and the election began on Wednesday, 30th. A great part of the night our Isle people kept drumming, shouting and firing of pistols and guns under the window where my wife lay, who had been brought to bed not three weeks. I had put the child to nurse over against my own house; the noise kept his nurse waking till one or two in the morning. Then they left off and his nurse, being heavy with sleep, overlaid the child. She waked and finding it dead, ran over to my house almost distracted, and calling my servants, threw it into their arms. They, as wise as she, ran with it to my wife, and before she was well awake, threw it cold and dead into hers. She composed herself as well as she could, and that day got it buried.

A clergyman met me in the castle yard, and told me to withdraw, for the Isle men intended me a mischief. Another told me he had heard near twenty of them say, 'If they got me in the castle yard they would squeeze my guts out' ... I went [home] by Gainsbro' and God preserved me.

When they knew I was got home, they sent the drum and mob, with guns etc., to compliment me till after midnight. One of them, passing by on Friday evening and seeing my children in the yard cried out, 'O ye devils! we will come and turn ye all out of doors a-begging shortly.' God convert them and forgive them!

All this, thank God, does not in the least sink my wife's spirits. For my own, I feel them disturbed and disordered...

S. Wesley[2]

Despite Samuel's words about his wife's spirits, the loss of this infant son must have been deeply distressing for Susanna, not least the traumatic experience of having him thrust into her arms, cold and dead, in the dark of night and before she was properly awake. We shall never know the full extent of this tragedy, for if this little boy had lived he might have grown up possessing abilities similar to those of his brothers, John and Charles, and have proved mighty as a preacher or a poet, or both.

Nor were these the only disappointments that lay in Samuel's path. He was promised a reward following his fulsome praise of the Duke of Marlborough in one of his poems. He was to be given the chaplaincy of an army regiment — a position that would seldom require him to be away from home, but which would provide him with an additional salary. But before he actually received any money from this source the position was taken away from him through the influence of his opponents.

On another occasion he had to travel to London to see a nobleman who then offered him a prebend — a stipend granted out of the estate of a cathedral — but once again he was prevented from taking up the offer through the action of his foes.

Back at Epworth his crop of flax was set on fire, his cattle were stabbed and wounded, his dog, a mastiff, was attacked and its leg nearly severed. It seemed that, whichever way he turned, he faced opposition and disappointment.

Among Wesley's creditors was a man to whom he owed £30. This man had him arrested, refused all negotiations and had him thrown into jail at Lincoln. We see a gentler side of Samuel's nature in a letter that he wrote from the prison:

> I thank God my wife was pretty well recovered, and churched some days before I was taken from her... One of my biggest concerns was my being forced to leave my poor lambs in the midst of so many wolves. But the great Shepherd is able to provide for them, and to preserve them. My wife bears it with that courage which becomes her, and which I expected from her.
>
> I don't despair of doing some good here ... and it may be I shall do more in this new parish than in my old; for I have leave to read prayers every morning and afternoon here in the prison, and to preach once a Sunday... And I'm getting acquainted with my brother jail-birds as fast as I can; and shall write to London to the Society for Propagating Christian Knowledge, who, I hope, will send me some books to distribute among them.[3]

In another letter from prison Samuel says, 'A jail is a paradise in comparison of the life I led before I came hither.' He goes on to list the several trials he had met with and states, 'I bless God my wife is less concerned with suffering them than I am in writing them.' Susanna sent him her wedding rings to sell so that he could pay the creditor, but he refused even to consider the suggestion and immediately returned them.

Letter from Samuel Wesley to Dr Sharpe during his imprisonment in Lincoln Castle, in which he says that Susanna sent him her rings to sell

Susanna found it more difficult to feed the family while Samuel was in prison. He says concerning the stabbing of his cattle that his enemies had 'endeavoured thereby to starve my poor family in my absence, my cows being all dried up by it, which was their chief subsistence...' They had been used to make butter and cheese from the milk, but now they were probably reduced to nothing but vegetables and grain. Some time later Susanna wrote, 'The late Archbishop of York once said to me when my master was in Lincoln Castle, "Tell me, Mrs Wesley, if you ever really wanted bread." "My lord," said I, "I will freely own to your grace that, strictly speaking, I never did want bread. But then I had so much care to get it before it was eat, and to pay for it after, as has often made it very unpleasant to me. And I think to have bread on such terms is the next degree of wretchedness to having none at all."'[4]

Various persons, learning of Samuel's imprisonment, sent sums of money to secure his release. There is no record stating precisely how long he was held, but his arrest took place in June 1705 and before the end of the year he was at home again.

Shortly after his release Samuel divulged a great plan that he had developed for the furtherance of foreign missions. He spoke of going to Surat in India, using that place as a centre and reaching out by travel or by correspondence to St Helena, China and Abyssinia and to the followers of the apostle Thomas 'who were in all parts of the Indian nation'. He would endeavour to learn the language of Hindoostan so that he might preach to the people in their native language. He also indicated his hope that the plan might interest the East India Company and that the queen might give it encouragement. He said, 'If one hundred pounds per annum might be allowed me, and forty I must pay my curate in my absence, I should be ready to venture my life, provided any way might be found to secure a subsistence for my family.'[5]

Nothing came of the plan, however. It reveals a commendable zeal for missionary endeavour on Samuel's part, but it also shows that he still wanted to escape from his troubles in England and to get away from Susanna and the children.

However, being obliged to remain in Epworth, Samuel did not neglect his ministry there. He was no doubt up early every morning and vitally active throughout the day. There were some 300 homes in the parish and during the thirty-eight years that he lived there he visited them all in order three times. It is claimed that he knew every parishioner and that the sick and dying were the objects of his special attention. In his visitation he wasted no time on trifles. He believed that since he was in holy orders he possessed authority over the people and when he entered a home he made his presence felt. He questioned both parents and children as to their religious behaviour: 'Who can say the prayers and catechisms? Who have been confirmed? Who have received the communion?' His manner could range from the kindly to the imperious. He was liked by some but feared by others.

His pulpit ministry apparently had a similar effect. Being a scholar, he laboured in the preparation of his sermons and manifestly gave his hearers substantial teaching. Yet we are told, 'The Sabbath congregations were exceedingly small. The communicants at the holy sacrament of the Supper seldom numbered twenty. The baptism of children was either totally neglected or so long delayed that the "monsters of men children brought to the font" made the minister's arm ache with their weight, while their "manful voices disturbed and alarmed the whole congregation".'[6]

Samuel held to the view that as a clergyman he was responsible to discipline his parishioners. This concept undoubtedly coloured much of what he said from the pulpit and we may be sure such statements aroused antagonism. He was especially severe in the case of persons known to have been guilty of adultery. He ordered them to be present at the Sunday morning service, and 'The criminal was seen standing for three successive Sabbaths, on the damp mud floor in the centre of the church, without shoes or stockings; bareheaded, covered with a white sheet, and shivering with cold. This was "doing penance" and the offender publicly stood forth as a warning to others...'[7] This practice had been discarded by most clergymen by this time, but Wesley retained it.

In 1709 an event took place which affected the lives of the entire Wesley family: the rectory was burned to the ground. Susanna told the story in a letter to her son Samuel:

Epworth, February 14th, 1708-9

Dear Sammy,

When I received your letter, wherein you complained of want of shirts, I little thought that in so short a space we should all be reduced to the same, and indeed a worse condition. I suppose you have already heard of the firing of our house, by what accident we cannot imagine; but the fire broke out about eleven or twelve at night, we being all in bed, nor did we perceive it till the roof of the corn-chamber fell upon your sister Hetty's bed... She awaked, and immediately ran to call your father... He says he heard some crying 'Fire!' in the street before, but did not apprehend where it was till he opened his door; he ... bade us all shift for life, for the roof was falling fast, and nothing but the thin wall kept the fire from the staircase.

We had no time to take our clothes... I called to Betty [a maidservant] to bring the children out of the nursery; she took up Patty, and left Jacky to follow her, but he going to the door and seeing all on fire, ran back again. We got the street door open, but the wind drove the flame with such violence, that none could stand against it. I tried thrice to break through, but was driven back. I made another attempt, and waded through the fire, which did me no other hurt than to scorch my legs and face. When I was in the yard I looked about for your father and the children; but, seeing none, concluded them all lost.

But, I thank God, I was mistaken! Your father carried sister Emily, Suky, and Patty into the garden; then, missing Jacky, he ran back into the house, to see if he could save him. He heard him miserably crying out in the nursery, and attempted several times to get upstairs, but was beat back by the flame; then he thought him lost, and commended his soul to God, and went to look after the rest. The child climbed up to the window, and called out to them in the yard; they got up to the casement, and pulled him out just as the roof fell into the chamber. Harry [the manservant] broke the glass in the parlour window, and threw out your sisters Mary and Hetty; and so, by God's great mercy, we all escaped. Do not be discouraged: God will provide for you.

Susanna Wesley[8]

The fire probably began in the fireplace chimney. Samuel said afterwards, 'We had been brewing, but had done all; every spark of fire quenched before five o'clock that evening — at least six hours before the house was on fire. Perhaps the chimney above might take fire (though it had been swept not long since) and break through into the thatch.'⁹

The entire rectory was consumed in the flames — the house, the furniture, Samuel's books, the parish records and all the family's possessions.

Susanna was eight months pregnant at the time of the fire. She and Samuel, with Charles, who was a child of two, went to live with parishioners in Epworth, and there, within a month, the baby Kezia was born. This was the last of Susanna's nineteen children. The others were placed in various homes and two, Sukey and Hetty, went to live with their Uncle Matthew, a prosperous physician in London.

Samuel quickly began the construction of a new rectory. He planned a house that was of solid brick and sufficiently large to serve his considerable family. The costs were partly supplied by the Ecclesiastical Commissioners, but a great deal of the expense, £400, fell to him. This responsibility set him still further in debt.

Many people have felt for Susanna in the many trials that she was called on to bear. But Samuel also deserves a share of our sympathy, even though many of his difficulties were of his own making. In the midst of all these trials he wrote 'A prayer for one in affliction and want' and in it he reveals his inner self, the essence of Samuel Wesley. Here it is:

O God, who art infinite in power, and compassion, and goodness, and truth, who hast promised in thy holy Word that thou wilt hear the prayer of the poor and the destitute ... look down, I beseech thee ... upon me, a miserable sinner, now lying under thy hand in great affliction and sorrow... I am weary of my groaning; my heart faileth me; the light of my eyes is gone from me; I sink in the deep waters and there is none to help me; yet I wait still upon thee, my God.

... I believe, O Lord, that thou who feedest the ravens, and clothest the lilies, wilt not neglect me (and mine); that thou wilt make good thy own unfailing promises, wilt give meat to them that fear thee, and be ever mindful of thy covenant. In the meantime let me not be querulous or impatient, or envious at the prosperity of the wicked, or judge uncharitably of those to whom thou hast given a larger portion of the good things of this life, nor be cruel to those who are in the same circumstances with myself. Let me never sink or despond under my heavy pressures and continued misfortunes...

Help me carefully to examine my life past; and if, by my own carelessness or imprudence, I have reduced myself into this low condition, let me be more deeply afflicted by it, but yet still hope in thy goodness, avoiding those failures whereof I have been formerly guilty... Teach us the emptiness of all things here below, wean us more and more from a vain world, fix our hearts more upon heaven, and help us forward in the right way that leads to everlasting life, through Jesus Christ our Lord, etc. Amen.[10]

There certainly were two sides to Samuel Wesley — one might almost say two personalities. Here in this prayer we see the better side, the man who recognizes his faults, admits them before God and prays that he may be given grace to overcome them. Here indeed is a kind and good and humbled man, who desires only to serve God.

The manner of high life being frivolous and depraved, no wonder that servants were neither wiser nor better than their employers. Complaints were universal of the arrogance, dishonesty, laziness, and luxury of valets and footmen; whilst charges against pert, mercenary, intriguing women servants were equally loud and numerous.

Such a condition of the natural character was a fruitful soil for superstition and credulity. Almost every old mansion was ghost-haunted, and almost every parish was tormented by a witch. Fortune-telling was a common and thriving occupation and quack doctors were, if possible, still more numerous than astrologers.

(Luke Tyerman, 1866).

7

The Wesleys Believe
Their House Is Haunted

In less than a year the rebuilding work on the rectory was completed. But the house was still in a very unfinished condition, though Samuel expressed his intention of having the rest of the work done as soon as his finances would permit.

The family returned and took up residence in their new home. They were clad in used clothing and the only furniture they now possessed was provided by the charity of neighbours. But other furniture was needed for even the most basic standard of living and though Samuel was already heavily in debt over the rebuilding of the house, it was imperative that further items should be purchased. So the debt grew even larger.

Susanna's task of training her children was also now made more difficult. She says, 'Never were children better disposed to piety ... till that fatal dispersion of them, after the fire, into several families. In those they were left at full liberty to converse with the servants, which before they had always been restrained from; and to run abroad and play with any children, good or bad. They soon learned to neglect a strict observation of the Sabbath, and got knowledge of several songs and bad things ... a clownish accent and many rude ways were learned, which were not reformed without some difficulty.'[1]

In an effort towards restoring the children to their former behaviour, Susanna arranged a special private conference with each child once a week. She said, 'On Monday I talk with Molly; on Tuesday with Hetty; Wednesday with Nancy; Thursday with Jacky; Friday with Patty; Saturday with Charles; and with Emilia and

The Old Rectory, Epworth. (This is the rectory which Samuel had built after the fire.)

Sukey together on Sunday.' This was important training, over and above the academic instruction they received in the school, and it enabled the mother to know her children individually and to show them the evil of the habits they had learned and teach them the better way of Christian practice. Here again her efforts met very largely with success.

About this time Samuel began a mighty literary undertaking: a commentary on the book of Job, written in Latin. He anticipated that it would be the chief literary accomplishment of his lifetime and that it would be such a financial success that it would enable him to pay off all his debts. He continued to labour at it till his death twenty-five years later, and even then it was not quite finished.

During 1712 Samuel had a curate named Inman to help him in the parish. This man, who normally preached only when Samuel was absent, usually held forth on the subject of the sinfulness of being in debt. On learning of this practice Samuel thought he would put him to the test and asked him to preach on an occasion when he would be present. Samuel also supplied the text: 'Without faith it is impossible to please God.' The curate began, 'Friends, faith is a most excellent virtue, and it produces other virtues also. In particular it makes a man pay his debts.' He then proceeded to rail against being in debt for some fifteen minutes. Nevertheless he was not discharged for publicly denouncing the rector's chief fault.

Inman is remembered especially for a series of events that took place in 1712 at a time when Samuel was in London. Susanna, whose soul had recently been stirred by reading an account of certain Danish missionaries, was not satisfied with seeing the people left with nothing but Inman's fatuous discourses. Since she was a woman and not allowed to preach, she began to read a sermon aloud from a book each Sunday afternoon. Using her kitchen, she read to her family and to any neighbours who came in, and soon the room was overflowing.

Inman, aroused by her success, wrote to Samuel telling him that she was conducting a conventicle — an illegal meeting. Samuel replied directly to Susanna, complaining and stating that she ought at least to have a man do the reading. She answered, 'You do not consider what a people these are. I do not think one man among them could read a sermon without spelling a good part of it.'² Again Samuel wrote, saying she ought to desist. But Susanna was almost defiant, asserting: 'If you do, after all, think fit to dissolve this

Susanna holding a meeting in the Rectory

assembly, do not tell me that you desire me to do it, for that will not satisfy my conscience; but send me your positive command, in such full and express terms as may absolve me from all guilt and punishment, for neglecting this opportunity of doing good, when you and I shall appear before the great and awful tribunal of our Lord Jesus Christ.'[3]

Samuel said no more. Susanna spoke of her audiences being many more than her kitchen could hold and she stated that they sometimes numbered as many as 200. When Samuel returned home he found his own Sunday congregations much increased and a new measure of good will in the parish as a result of Susanna's services.

Two years later, in 1714, John, now a boy of eleven, left home to attend Charterhouse School in London. Besides having been in his mother's school since he was five, he had been given instruction in Latin and Greek and the literature of those languages by his father. He was in an excellent measure prepared for the studies that now lay before him. Although the sons of many of the aristocracy were enrolled at Charterhouse, like most schools it was a place of bullying and rough behaviour, but in spite of the sheltered life he had known at home, John proved well able to withstand the treatment to which he was subjected on his arrival there.

At about this time, a series of strange events took place at the Epworth rectory. Susanna and Samuel and their family became convinced that their house was haunted. The parents had both already manifested their belief in ghosts, apparitions and hauntings. Samuel had declared his certainty of the reality of the spirit world, saying that 'The soul, after its separation from the body, may again be clothed with some sort of aerial, fiery or cloudy vehicle, and be visible to our senses.'[4] We also recall that, following her father's death, Susanna had spoken of his presence still inhabiting the house and of frequently communing with his spirit.

On the first day of December 1715, a new maid, Nanny Marshall, claimed to have heard a strange and terrible noise in the house. It was, she said, like the dismal groans of a man in the pains of dying. Then two of the Wesley sisters, Sukey, aged twenty-one, and Anne, fourteen, stated that they heard something rushing by on the outside of the house, followed by three knocks, repeated three times, inside. Two nights later Emilia, who was twenty-three, thought she heard the sound of several bottles being broken and of a large lump of coal being dumped onto the kitchen floor, but when she examined the area she could find no broken glass and no pieces of coal. She also discovered that the large mastiff watchdog had slept through the time when the sounds were made. Then a youth, who lived in the house and did manual work for the Wesleys, told of hearing someone walking up and down the stairs, trailing a long garment and gobbling like a turkey cock. He also stated that he saw something that looked like a rabbit run out of 'a hole in the copper', spin round three times and run off, but it eluded his attempts to catch it.

Samuel himself heard none of these strange happenings. At the end of two weeks of disturbances the girls told him about them, but at first he gave little heed to their report, stating that the noises were the result of trickery by themselves or by their lovers. Susanna believed the noises were made by rats and she had a neighbour come in the daytime and sound a horn throughout the house to drive them away.

But after another week the noises were no longer heard only by the girls. The parents began to hear them too.

First, Samuel and Susanna were startled by hearing nine loud knocks. Samuel said, however, that they may have come from outside the house. Two days later Emilia took Susanna into the nursery, where she heard noises under the bed. She also saw an animal like a badger without a head run across the room and hide under Emilia's skirts, On another night Samuel and Susanna were awakened by noises so violent that sleep was impossible. They got up and went through the house but, repeatedly, the sound seemed to come from the room they had just left.

Samuel soon took over the search himself and he acted with his usual determination. He thought he heard a rattling among a number of bottles and then the sound of several coins being poured out at Susanna's waist and jingling down to her feet. Wanting a witness to the strange events that were going on in the rectory he asked a fellow-clergyman, the Rev. Joseph Hoole from Haxey, to come and spend the night with him. Wesley and Hoole went through the house together and, hearing the usual tappings, Samuel was about to shoot his pistol in the direction from which they came, when Hoole urged him not to do so, stating that a spirit could not be hurt by a bullet.

Wesley states that he defied the spirit, challenging it with the words: 'Thou deaf and dumb devil, why dost thou frighten children that cannot answer thee? Come to *me* in my study that am a man!' Immediately it replied using the same sequence of knocks as he himself used when he came to his outside door in the night and wanted to let Susanna know that he was there. On the next night Samuel said that as he entered his study the door was thrust back on him with such force as almost to knock him to the floor. He called on his daughter Anne to stand by him and he once again challenged the spirit to speak. But it made no sound.

Samuel then said to Anne, 'Spirits love darkness; put out the candle and perhaps then it will speak.' Despite being left in total darkness, Anne courageously obeyed. He repeated his challenge, yet all remained silent. But he continued the contest, telling Anne, 'Two Christians are an overmatch for the devil; go downstairs, and it may be, when I am left alone, it will speak.' He waited but still he heard nothing. Then, supposing that the spirit's visits to the home indicated that his son Sammy in London had died, he solemnly charged it, 'If thou art the spirit of my son Samuel, I pray thee knock three knocks and no more.' There was no response.

For the next twenty-seven days no noises were heard, but then they began again. While the family were at their devotions knocks were heard during the petition for the king, and when the prayer was concluded, the 'Amen' was accompanied by a mighty thump. The next day Samuel omitted the prayer for the king and there was no sound, but the following day, when he again mentioned the monarch, the tappings were heard once more.

On one occasion Samuel's plate began dancing on the table during supper, and he said that on several nights the latch was lifted on his door. Another time Emilia attempted to hold the latch on the back door of the kitchen, but she claimed it was still lifted and the door pushed violently against her. Three times Samuel declared he was pushed, either by a door or by an unknown force which drove him against his desk. As a rule, the noises began at a time when the wind was strong; it whistled loudly around the outside of the house, and inside it rattled the pewter, banged the doors and moved the curtains.

Samuel believed the girls were frightened by the spirit. This was possibly true when the noises first began, but after a while they joked about it. They called it 'Old Jeffrey', the name of a former occupant of the rectory, and after going to bed they would say, 'Old Jeffrey is coming; it's time to go to sleep.' They also reported an occasion when three girls were in the nursery and the bed was lifted up to a considerable height. Anne was sitting on it and said, 'Surely Old

Jeffrey won't run away with me!' It seems that it had become a cause of merriment for them.

Virtually all of these supposedly supernatural events took place at night and the only light was the feeble illumination from a candle. Moreover, nothing was seen apart from the reports of the rabbit and the headless badger, and the only sign of the ghost's presence was noises — chiefly knocks — and these the family said sometimes came from outside the house. Samuel attempted to get the ghost to speak, but there was never any response, except for a squeak on one occasion.

This series of happenings was not of long duration. It began on the first of December and apparently continued for three weeks, then was interrupted for twenty-seven days, began again and came to an end early in February. It stopped as suddenly as it had started.

The Wesleys attributed a particular significance to these goings-on. At first the girls were afraid to tell their father about the noises because they feared the sounds indicated that either he or one of their brothers was about to die. Susanna also expressed her fear that they portended the death of one of her sons. And as we have seen, Samuel addressed the ghost demanding, 'If thou art the spirit of my son Samuel, knock three times.'

So what was the real cause of these strange events? At that time the vast majority of people everywhere were fully convinced that ghosts really existed and all the Wesleys were strongly of that conviction. Because of their background, when they heard the unaccountable sounds in the darkness, night after night, they readily believed them to be supernatural. It was more natural for them, even though they were highly intelligent people, to accept this view than to reject it.

Dr Joseph Priestly, who was in possession of the letters written by the Wesley family concerning this matter, 'thought the whole affair was a trick of the servants, assisted by some of the neighbours, for the purpose of puzzling the family and amusing themselves'. One or two people inside the house, conniving with others outside, could have produced the knocking and this, combined with the strong winds, could have caused the superstitious family to believe them to be the activities of a ghost. The sudden way in which the phenomenon started and stopped lends credence to the view that it was the work of a human hand.

Who on the inside would have been involved in such trickery?

The young manservant, Robin Brown, or the new maidservant, Nanny Marshall, may have taken some part in these events, but not enough is known about them to speculate further.

On the other hand, a member of the family may possibly have been involved. This was the daughter Hetty. At the time of the fire which destroyed the rectory Hetty was a girl of thirteen and she had spent the following year with her Uncle Matthew, a successful physician in London. Freed from the control of her parents, she had enjoyed the greater liberty in her uncle's house and when she returned to Epworth she felt the restraints under which she was placed at home. Since she was now nineteen and beautiful in face and figure, young men were attracted to her company and her father's suggestion that the noises were the result of his daughters entertaining their lovers would have applied to Hetty more than to any of the others. She was full of animal spirits and, being given to mischief, she could well have agreed with one or two young men to play tricks on her father.

It may be significant that, although there is a written statement on the ghost affair from virtually every other member of the family, there is none from her. Either she left nothing about it, or whatever she wrote was deemed inadmissible and was destroyed. We shall look in more detail at the character of Hetty in a later chapter.

Dr Adam Clarke, a personal associate of John Wesley, reported the following possible explanation: 'One night, after the family had gone to bed, the maidservant was finishing her work in the back kitchen, when she was startled by a noise, looked up, and saw a man working himself through a trough which communicated between the sink-stone within and a cistern without.' Clarke goes on to say that the servant struck the escaping intruder on the head, that Samuel shouted and threw the fire-irons down the stairs and that the man left a trail of blood for some distance.[5] This concept agrees with the idea that the neighbours were involved in perpetrating the trickery.

Although John was a boy of only thirteen and was at school in London at the time, this series of events had a lasting effect on him. He was certain that it was supernatural and stated that he considered it to be God's judgement on his father for having forsaken Susanna and her children fourteen years earlier. It also burned into John's consciousness the certainty that the spirits of departed ones are alive and although unseen are active among mankind.

Charles, who was also at school in London at the time, makes no mention of Old Jeffrey, leading one to wonder if he seriously believed in his existence.

Susanna and Samuel, together with their children, were creatures of the century in which they lived, when it came to their conviction of the reality of the spirit world. The vast majority of their contemporaries would have joined them in this superstitious belief.[6]

Several writers have made suggestions as to the identity of 'Old Jeffrey'. 'Coleridge discovers in the Wesley family "an angry and damnatory predetermination" to believe in the ghost... Dr Salmon accuses Hetty Wesley of playing tricks on her family and producing all the noises... Priestly offers the theory of imposture by servants and neighbours; Isaac Taylor resolves "Old Jeffrey" into a monkey-like "performing droll" of a spirit. Mr Wesley had preached for several Sundays against the "cunning men" of the neighbourhood whom the ignorant peasants used to consult as wizards; and Andrew Lang thinks the performances of "Old Jeffrey" were the revenge taken by these "cunning men".'[7]

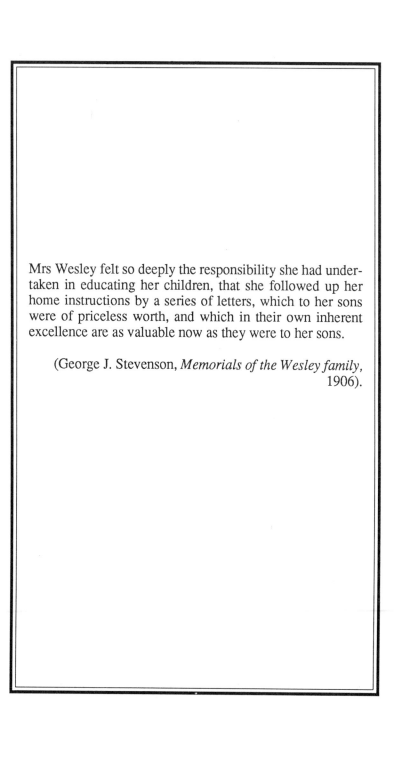

Mrs Wesley felt so deeply the responsibility she had under-
taken in educating her children, that she followed up her
home instructions by a series of letters, which to her sons
were of priceless worth, and which in their own inherent
excellence are as valuable now as they were to her sons.

(George J. Stevenson, *Memorials of the Wesley family*,
1906).

8

Susanna's Advanced Education
of Her Sons

We have seen that the Wesley sons left home to obtain further schooling while they were still boys. Samuel, after attending a regular school in Epworth, was sent at the age of thirteen to the St Peter's Classical School adjoining Westminster Abbey. John attended his mother's classes in the rectory till he was eleven, when he was sent to London to attend the Charterhouse School. Charles likewise attended his mother's school, and at the age of nine he went to live with his brother Samuel and to attend the Westminster School.

While the boys were at home, over and above the instruction received from their mother, they were also taught to some extent by their father. Samuel instructed his sons in Latin and Greek and in classical literature and thus he laid the foundation on which they built solid structures of learning in Westminster, Charterhouse and Oxford.

Once the sons left home, however, Susanna took it upon herself to continue instructing them, doing this in a number of letters. The contents of some of these letters were manifestly above the understanding of young boys, but they showed them there was an advanced learning available in life. She instructed them in religious truth and philosophized about God and man, about right and wrong and numerous other elements of human life. Some of her reasonings may be difficult for modern readers to grasp as well, but they are presented here as evidence of the unusual intellect of the woman with whom we are dealing.

Susanna wrote especially to her son Sammy. She perhaps felt

that since she did not begin her school in the rectory till after he had left home she needed to make up some of the training he had missed. The opening paragraphs of one of her first letters to him read:

Epworth, March 11, 1704

Dear Sammy,

The eternal law with respect to man is called 'the law of reason'; when it is more clearly explained by revelation, 'divine'; when it orders natural agents which obey it willingly, yet constantly and regularly, we style it 'the law of nature and instinct'. And you may here take notice that in the observation of this law consists the happiness of all creatures; and it is only that which conserves the being and composes the harmony which we observe in the works of the Creator...

Now by what has been said you may learn that a law is a rule of an action. Now where this is taken from the nature of things, and respects rational, voluntary agents, it is called 'moral'; and our agreement or conformity to it, 'moral virtue'. The law of reason (which is the foundation of morality) is also, and not improperly, called 'the law of nature'; because it is not only a rule of action to rational, voluntary agents, but it is a rule we are capable of discovering by our natural light without the assistance of revelation; so you plainly perceive you are obliged, as a man, to observe all the precepts of morality, or natural religion, though you had never heard of Christ or Moses. I cannot here enumerate all the particulars of this great law; I shall only hint at those that are most obvious and easy to be understood. I intend you an entire discourse upon it when I have more time.[1]

Susanna's 'only hinting at' such things went on for another 315 lines!

Her next letter to Sammy was written some five months later. She had been ill, but was now largely recovered and she said, 'I shall be employing my thoughts on useful subjects to you when I have time, for I desire nothing in this world so much as to have my children well instructed in the principles of religion, that they may walk in the narrow way which alone leads to happiness. Particularly I am concerned for you, who were, before your birth, dedicated to the service of the sanctuary, that you may be an ornament of that church of which you are a member...'[2]

In another letter to Sammy, Susanna enlarged upon the Scripture, 'Let your light so shine before men that they may see your good works, and glorify your Father which is in heaven,' telling him, 'The mind of a Christian should be always composed, temperate, free from all extremes of mirth or sadness, and always disposed to hear the voice of God's Holy Spirit.'

Like virtually all mankind in that day, Susanna and Samuel were not teetotallers regarding the use of alcoholic drink. Pure water was difficult to obtain in many places and people resorted to the practice of brewing to make sure that all impurities were removed. The Wesleys brewed in their kitchen, and John, during his ministry, considered himself a connoisseur on the taste of good drink.

However, Susanna sought to warn Sammy of the dangers of over-indulgence. Writing to him on 22 May 1706 she stated, 'Two glasses cannot hurt you, provided they contain no more than those commonly used.' Then she went on to admonish, 'Have a care; stay at the third glass; I consider you have an obligation to strict temperance, which all have not — I mean your designation for holy orders. Remember, under the Jewish economy it was ordained by God himself that the snuffers of the temple should be perfect gold; from which we may infer that those who are admitted to serve at the altar ... ought themselves to be most pure, and free from scandalous action...'[3]

Writing to Sammy a year later, earnestly desirous that he be saved, Susanna presented her concept of how to be saved — her concept of the way of salvation. After urging the reason for which he was created, 'to know, love and obey God,' she said,

> This life is nothing in comparison of eternity; so very inconsiderable, and withal so wretched, that it is not worth-while to be, if we were to die as the beasts. What mortal would sustain the pains, the wants, the disappointments, the cares, and thousands of calamities we must often suffer here? But when we consider this as a probationary state ... and that if we wisely behave ourselves here, if we purify our souls from all corrupt and inordinate affections, if we can, by the divine assistance, recover the image of God (moral goodness),

which we lost in Adam, and attain to a heavenly temper and disposition of mind, full of the love of God, etc., then we justly think that this life is an effect of the inconceivable goodness of God towards us...

I have such a vast inexpressible desire of your salvation, and such dreadful apprehensions of your failing in a work of so great importance; and do moreover know by experience how hard a thing it is to be a Christian, that I cannot for fear, I cannot but most earnestly press you and conjure you, over and over again, to give the most earnest heed to what you have already learned, lest at any time you let slip the remembrance of your final happiness, or forget what you have to do in order to attain it.[4]

As much as we may rejoice in the extraordinary earnestness manifested by Susanna in seeking Sammy's salvation, we cannot but regret that she did not know the 'finished' work of Christ, and the assurance of salvation which God grants to 'him that believeth'. How different was this concept of Susanna's from that experienced by Charles and John following their conversions in May 1738!

It is evident that Susanna, holding so strongly to the doctrine of salvation by works, and depending on human reason rather than on divine revelation, would have rejected the teaching that man's salvation begins with God. This rejection she had taught to her children. John wrote to her on this matter when he was preparing for ordination. He confessed that he could not accept the seventeenth section of the *Articles of Religion*, which so plainly declares the Church of England's belief in the doctrine of predestination and shows it to be a beautiful and comforting doctrine.

Susanna replied to John, but she did not deal with predestination as presented in the Prayer Book. She dealt with it only in an exceptionally extreme and distorted sense, and nowhere did she refer to the several Scriptures which declare the doctrine nor did she treat of what was stated in the Article. Three of her letters to him reveal her views on this subject. In the first she says, 'The case stands thus: this life is a probation, wherein eternal happiness or misery are proposed to our choice; the one as a reward of a virtuous, the other as the consequence of a vicious life.'

In the second letter she asserts, 'I do firmly believe that God from all eternity hath elected some to everlasting life, but then I humbly conceive that this election is founded in his foreknowledge, according to Romans 8:29,30.'⁵ She then cites these two verses, assuming that God 'foreknew' that some men, when presented with the gospel, would accept it. Nowhere does she mention the truth that man is 'dead in trespasses and sins' — that he could do nothing and that God 'foreknew' what he himself would do. Nor does she show any understanding of the biblical use of the word 'foreknowledge' as a term indicating God's affection and love towards mankind.

We should also notice a letter she wrote to John in 1727. He was then twenty-four, a tutor at Oxford and a Fellow of Lincoln College. But for three years he had been frequently in the company of a circle of cultivated young women in nearby Cotswold villages and Susanna wrote informing him about the enjoyments but also the dangers of human love. She stated, for instance, 'Ah, my dear son, did you with me stand on the verge of life, and saw before your eyes a vast expanse, an unlimited duration of being, which you might shortly enter upon, you can't conceive how all the inadvertencies, mistakes and sins of youth would rise up to your view; and how different the sentiments of sensitive pleasures, the desire of sexes, the pernicious friendships of the world, would be then from what they are now, while health is entire and seems to promise many years of life.'⁶

In another letter to John, written on 14 May 1727, Susanna stated, 'I must confess I never yet met with such an accurate definition of the passion of love as fully satisfied me. It is indeed commonly defined as "a desire of union with a known or apprehended good". But this directly makes love and desire the same thing; which, on a close inspection I perceive they are not, for this reason: desire is strongest and acts most vigorously when the beloved object is distant, or apprehended unkind or displeased; whereas, when the union is attained, and fruition perfect, complacency, delight and joy fill the soul of the lover, while desire lies quiescent; which plainly shows (at least to me) that desire of union is an *effect* of love, and not love *itself*.'⁷

Thus did Susanna instruct John, but there is little evidence of any effect of her words in his own life. His two love affairs — one with Sophia Hopkey and the other with Grace Murray — and his marriage were not exactly models of understanding!

Susanna also wrote manuals for her children, and these she considered to be simplified handbooks on Christian doctrine.

Most important of all, she wrote an exposition of the Apostles' Creed. She went through this historic statement of belief point after point, and we shall consider her concept of faith when we come to look at her letters to Charles after his conversion in 1738. For the present we shall notice her portrayal of the passion of Christ. In reference to his suffering in Gethsemane, in the judgement hall and upon the cross, her solemn words are:

He must be forsaken of his Father in the midst of his torments, which made him thrice so earnestly repeat his petition that if it were possible that cup might pass from him. But the full complement of his sufferings we may suppose to be that he did at that time actually sustain the whole weight of that grief and sorrow which was due to the justice of God for the sins of the whole world. And this, we may believe, caused that inconceivable agony when his sweat was as great drops of blood falling down to the ground.

And though his torments were so inexpressibly great, yet the Son of Man must suffer many things. He must be betrayed by one disciple, denied by another, and forsaken by all. And as he had suffered in his soul by the most intense grief and anguish, so he had to suffer in his body the greatest bitterness of corporeal pains, which the malice and rage of his enemies could inflict upon it. And now the Sovereign Lord and Judge of all men is haled before the tribunal of his sinful creatures: the pure and unspotted Son of God who could do no wrong, neither could guile be found in his mouth, accused by his presumptuous slaves of no less a crime than blasphemy...

But though the corporeal pains occasioned by the thorns, the scourging, by the piercing those nervous and most sensible parts of his most sacred body, were wrought up to an inexpressible degree of torture; yet were they infinitely surpassed by the anguish of his soul when there was (but after what manner we cannot conceive) a sensible withdrawing of the comfortable presence of Deity, which caused that loud and impassioned exclamation: 'My God, my God, why hast thou forsaken me?'

And now it is finished and he who could not die but by his own voluntary act of resigning life, gave up his pure and spotless life into the hands of his almighty Father.[8]

Susanna continued in this way till she made an exposition of the whole of the Apostles' Creed. It would be well if this treatise, which she presented to her daughter Sukey and which she intended should be read by all her children, was available as a single item for both children and their parents to read today.

Samuel Wesley also wrote to his boys with a view towards encouraging them intellectually and advancing them spiritually. For instance, in his first letter to his son Samuel he stated,

> Most of what I write to you will be the result of my own dear-bought experience ... and you may expect a letter once a month, at least, or once a fortnight; and I hope, in mere civility, you will sometimes write again.
>
> And I shall begin, as I ought, with piety, strictly so called, or your duty towards God, which is the foundation of all happiness; I mean your immediate duty to him, both in public and private; as for your morals I shall send my thoughts hereafter.

The father went on, reasoning with his son about the person of God, and he closed, saying,

> I commend you to God's gracious protection, and would have you always remember that he sees and loves you. Your mother will write soon to you. We are all well.
>
> I am your affectionate father,
>
> Samuel Wesley.[9]

In another letter to this son, Samuel praised Susanna:

> You know what you owe to one of the best of mothers ... often reflect on the tender and peculiar love which your mother has always expressed towards you, the deep afflic-tion, both of body and mind, which she underwent for you, both before and after your birth; the particular care she took of your education when she struggled with so many pains and infirmities; and, above all, the wholesome and sweet

motherly advice and counsel which she has often given you
to fear God, to take care of your soul, as well as your learning,
to shun all vicious practices and bad examples ... as well as
those valuable letters she wrote to you...
   You will not forget to evidence this by supporting and
comforting her in her age ... and doing nothing which may
justly displease and grieve her, or show you unworthy of such
a mother...
   In short, reverence and love her as much as you will... For
though I should be jealous of any other rival in your heart, yet
I will not be of her: the more duty you pay her and the more
frequently and kindly you write to her, the more will you
please

        your affectionate father,

                                        Samuel Wesley[10]

   The attitude manifested by Samuel in these letters to his son is
indicative of the better side of his nature. This undoubtedly was
evident, along with his native wit, in many of his activities, but
although he could be jovial and pleasant, he could also be dictatorial
and severe. 'I allow no rivals in my kingdom!' he once asserted to
John, and this declaration was true in his home and in his church.
   We especially notice the way he praises Susanna in the letter just
quoted. She was more than worthy of the commendations he gave
her and he very rightly desired that his children should never fail to
show their love for her.
   Thus, added to Susanna's efforts to educate her sons, there were
also these endeavours on the part of Samuel. The boys went to their
special schools well grounded in basic classical knowledge and
upon this they built the scholarship that characterized all of their
later lives.
   The girls, though left at home and denied the privileges accorded
to their brothers, benefited, nevertheless, from their father's learning, as well as from their mother's daily instruction, together with
her watchful admonition and her constant example.

'Is Mr Samuel Annesley on board?'

Captain Bewes rubbed his chin. He had grown suddenly grave. 'I beg your pardon,' said he, 'but are you a kinswoman of Mr Annesley's?'

'I am his sister, sir.'

'Then I'll have to ask you to step on board, ma'am.'

'Is — is he ill?' Mrs Wesley stammered... 'We heard he had taken passage with you.'

'Why, so he did; and, to the best of my knowledge he sailed. It's a serious matter, ma'am, and we're all at our wits' ends over it; but the fact is — Mr Annesley has disappeared.'

(Sir Arthur Quiller-Couch, *Hetty Wesley*, 1903).

9

The Loss of Samuel Annesley

A record of only one member of the large family in which Susanna was born has come down to us. That was of her brother, Samuel Annesley.

In 1683 Annesley and his wife went to India. The East India Company was vigorously promoting business with England, and capable, diligent efforts were bringing large rewards. Annesley, an enterprising young man, was determined to make his fortune.

The Wesleys' daughter Susanna was known to the family as Sukey. Her uncle Samuel, learning in India of her winsome personality, promised that when he became rich he would do handsomely by her. And he apparently expressed his intention of providing well for the rest of the Wesley girls and for their mother.

During the long years of their poverty the family had looked forward to Annesley's return. They bore with their worn-out clothing and the lack of variety in their diet, waiting for the day when he would sail into port and would fulfil his generous promises.

In order to understand the position of the Wesley girls, we must realize that conditions regarding employment for young women were very different then from what they are today. Class distinction was widely prevalent throughout England and although these girls might perform farm labours at home, milking cows and feeding sheep, they had about them a quality and a presence that rendered it out of the question for them to hire themselves out as servants in someone else's home. The only positions open to them were those of a teacher in a girls' school or a companion to some well-to-do lady.

The other alternative was that of being married. Although all manner of youths from Epworth and the area round about sought the company of the Wesley girls, few, if any of them, possessed the qualities that rendered them suitable to become lifelong partners to these extraordinary young women. Accordingly, as the years came and went, despite their temporary friendships, each was waiting till some young man of adequate standing, sufficient enterprise and pious character came into her life and won her heart.

In the meantime, while they worked in the house and on the farm, they anticipated the day when Samuel Annesley would return from India and would supply them, as they expected, with some of the things they had lacked so long. But over the years, relations between Susanna and her brother changed for the worse.

Needing someone to handle his affairs in England, Annesley wrote to Samuel Wesley, suggesting that he undertake this task, and no doubt offering to pay him well for doing so. However, Susanna raised certain objections to the scheme. She stated that her husband was too far removed from London to oversee the business adequately, and also that he might prove unfit to make decisions in commercial affairs. His ability to perform correctly the collecting and spending of money, she said, was open to question. But Wesley still agreed to serve as the agent for his brother-in-law.

The arrangement did not work well. As Susanna had predicted, Wesley proved inefficient in business decisions and in financial matters. After a time Annesley placed his affairs in the hands of another man, but he seems also to have been so incensed that he declared he would reconsider his intention to assist the girls and Susanna.

This proved a serious disappointment, especially to Sukey, to whom he had made a definite promise of provision. Under the shock of it she threw herself into a hasty marriage. Her husband, Richard Ellison, came from a well-to-do family from whom he received a considerable inheritance, but he was 'course, vulgar and immoral' and severely dominating in his manner, and he speedily made Sukey's life almost unbearable.

Further correspondence also took place between Annesley and Susanna. None of his letters have been retained, but we have one of hers to him. Writing in 1722, she said,

Sir,

The unhappy differences between you and Mr Wesley have prevented my writing for some years ... but feeling life ebb apace, and having a desire to be at peace with all men, especially you, before my exit, I have ventured to send one letter more, hoping you will give yourself the trouble to read it without prejudice.

I am, I believe, got on the right side of fifty, infirm and weak; yet old as I am, since I have taken my husband 'for better, for worse,' I'll take my residence with him: 'where he lives, will I live; and where he dies will I die; and there will I be buried. God do so unto me, and more also, if ought but death part him and me.'

Confinement is nothing to one that by sickness is compelled to spend a great part of her time in a chamber; and I sometimes think that, if it were not on account of Mr Wesley and the children, it would be perfectly indifferent to my soul whether she ascended to the supreme Origin of being from a jail or a palace, for God is everywhere...

Upon the best observation I could ever make, I am induced to believe that it is much easier to be contented without riches than with them. It is so natural for a rich man to make his gold his god ... it is so very difficult not to trust in, not to depend on it, for support and happiness, that I do not know one rich man in the world with whom I would exchange conditions.

You say, 'I hope you have recovered your loss by fire long since.' No; and it is to be doubted, never shall. Mr Wesley rebuilt his house in less than a year; but nearly thirteen years are elapsed since it was burned, yet it is not half furnished, nor his wife and children half clothed to this day. It is true that by the benefactions of his friends, together with what he had himself, he paid the first; but the latter is not paid yet, or, what is much the same, money which was borrowed for clothes and furniture is yet unpaid.

You go on, 'My brother's living of £300 a year, as they tell me.' *They?* Who? I wish those who say so were compelled to make it so. It may as truly be said that his living is £10,000 a year as £300. I have, sir, formerly laid before you the true state of our affairs. I have told you that the living was always let for £160 a year; that taxes, poor assessments, subrents, tenths, procurations, synodals, etc., took up nearly £30 of that moiety, so that there needs no great skill in arithmetic to compute what remains.

What we shall or shall not need hereafter God only knows; but at present there hardly ever was a greater coincidence of unprosperous events in one family than is now in ours. I am rarely in good health; Mr Wesley declines apace; my dear Emily, who in my present exigencies would exceedingly comfort me, is compelled to go to service in Lincoln, where she is a teacher in a boarding school; my second daughter, Sukey, a pretty woman, and worthy a better fate, when, by your last unkind letters, she perceived that all her hopes in you were frustrated, rashly threw herself upon a man (if a man he may be called who is little inferior to the apostate angels in wickedness) that is not only her plague, but a constant affliction to the family. Oh, sir! oh, brother! happy, thrice happy are you, happy is my sister, that buried your children in infancy! secure from temptation, secure from guilt, secure from want or shame, or loss of friends! They are safe beyond the reach of pain or sense of misery: being gone hence nothing can touch them further. Believe me, sir, it is better to mourn ten children dead than one living; and I have buried many. But here I must pause awhile.

The other children, though wanting neither industry nor capacity for business, we cannot put to any, by reason we have neither money nor friends to assist us in doing it; nor is there a gentleman's family near us in which we can place them, unless as common servants, and that even yourself would not think them fit for, if you saw them... Innumerable are other uneasinesses, too tedious to mention; insomuch that, with my own indisposition, my master's infirmities, the absence of my eldest, the ruin of my second daughter, and the inconceivable distress of all the rest, I have enough to turn a stronger head than mine.[1]

Annesley had suggested that Wesley had not been entirely honest in his financial dealings, to which Susanna replied:

These things are unkind, very unkind. Add not misery to affliction: if you will not reach out a friendly hand to support, yet I beseech you, forbear to throw water on a people already sinking.

But I shall go on with your letter to me. You proceed:

'When I come home' — oh, would to God that might ever be!
— 'should any of your daughters want me' — as I think they
will not — 'I shall do as God enables me!' I must answer this
with a sigh from the bottom of my heart...

You go on: 'My brother has one invincible obstacle to my
business, his distance from London.' Sir, you may please to
remember I put you in mind of this long since... 'Another
remora is, these matters are out of his way.' That is a remora
indeed, and ought to have been considered on both sides
before he entered upon your business; for I am verily persuaded that that, and that alone, has been the cause of any
mistakes or indavertency he has been guilty of, and the true
reason why God had not blessed him with desired success.

'He is apt to rest upon deceitful promises.' Would to God
that neither he, nor I, nor any of our children, had ever trusted
to deceitful promises! But it is a right-hand error, and I hope
God will forgive us all...

'He is not fit for worldly business.' This I likewise assent
to, and must own I was mistaken when I did think him fit for
it; my own experience has convinced me that he is one of
those who, our Saviour saith, 'are not so wise in their
generation as the children of this world'.

And did I not know that Almighty Wisdom hath views and
ends in fixing the bounds of our habitation, which are out of
our ken, I should think it a thousand pities that a man of his
brightness and rare endowments of learning and useful
knowledge in relation to the church of God should be confined to an obscure corner of the country where his talents are
buried, and he determined to a way of life for which he is not
so well qualified as I could wish...

I shall not detain you any longer — not so much as to
apologize for the tedious length of this letter...

I am,
your obliged and most obedient servant and sister,

Susanna Wesley[2]

Susanna is as much out of patience in this letter as in anything we
have from her pen. She is incensed with her brother's going back on

his word to her daughter Sukey and makes it plain that Sukey had trusted him and that he had disappointed her and also all of her sisters. Susanna's assertion that she would stay with her husband is probably an indication that Annesley had suggested that her wisest course would be to leave him. There is a fire in this letter that we see nowhere else in Susanna Wesley.

Although we have no document to confirm this, we have reason to believe that Annesley replied to Susanna's letter and that he apologized to some extent for his previous strictures. He also apparently stated that he would shortly be returning to England and urged Susanna to meet his vessel when it docked. Accordingly we find John writing to his brother Samuel, 'Tell me as near as you can how soon my uncle is expected in England and my mother in London.'[3]

Despite the enfeebled condition referred to in Susanna's letter, she summed up sufficient strength to take the arduous trip to London. The journey from Lincolnshire would mean five or six days of travelling with a stop at an inn during each night. There was considerable cost involved, but we must assume that the opportunity to get away from Epworth for a time and to revisit the scenes of her childhood revived her physically. Charles speaks of her delight in walking about London, viewing again the areas she had known as a child.

Having repaired the breach with her brother and having journeyed from Epworth to London to meet him, Susanna naturally looked forward to his arrival. The vessel on which he had left India docked in London on the appointed day. But, strange to say, Annesley was nowhere to be found. His personal goods were in his cabin as he had left them, but the officers of the ship knew nothing as to the cause of his disappearance. It is highly probable that he was murdered and his body thrown overboard.

Annesley had apparently made his fortune. John Wesley 'used to tell his nephews [sons of Charles], "You are heirs to a large property in India, if you can find it out; for my uncle is said to have been very prosperous."'[4]

Accordingly, bearing this sad news, Susanna journeyed back to Epworth. She went on suffering her pain and weakness, meeting the family's constant poverty, witnessing her husband's physical deterioration and bearing his increasing temper. She hoped her girls would find suitable men to marry, and anticipated the day when

John and Charles would be in holy orders and would be able to assist their parents.

Life had brought trial after trial and disappointment after disappointment for Susanna, but the greatest difficulty of all was the one she was now about to face — the tragedy involving her daughter Hetty.

In her later years Mrs Wright [Hetty Wesley] was an elegant woman, with great refinement of manners. She had the traces of beauty in her countenance, with the appearance of being broken-hearted.

(Dr Adam Clarke, a personal friend of John Wesley).

10

The Tragedy of Daughter Hetty

Susanna named her fifth daughter Mehetabel, but the family called her Hetty.

Born in 1697, from her early days Hetty seemed exceptionally bright and particularly capable. At the age of five she began to attend her mother's school, but her father, realizing that she possessed extraordinary qualities, gave her a form of education that he gave to none of his other daughters. This was instruction in the classics and by the time she was nine she was able to read Greek and Latin and had some knowledge of the literature of those languages. During the months that followed, because she wrote a beautiful hand, he had her assist him by transcribing his commentary on the book of Job. But her chief talent lay in composing poetry, a gift inherited from her father, but which rose to new heights in her.

Hetty's intelligence, however, was combined with unusual liveliness. We are told that 'From childhood she was vivacious and sprightly, full of mirth, good humour and clean wit.' She was the kind of girl who, because of her high animal spirits, possessed a tendency to mischief and this inclination threatened to outrun her judgement and to bring her into difficulties.

As we saw earlier, when the rectory was destroyed by fire, Hetty, then a girl of twelve, and Sukey, who was fourteen, went to live with their uncle Matthew in London. Matthew was a well-to-do physician and in living with him and his wife the girls had virtually none of the restrictions that they had known under their parents. After well over a year, they returned to Epworth, but, experiencing once more the poverty and the lack of the many diversions they had enjoyed in London, they found life dull and boring.

This was their condition when the mysterious incidents occurred in the rectory that were attributed to a ghost. It may be worth noting in this connection that Hetty, who by that time was nineteen, was usually the last one to go to bed at night, for her father had her sit up to take his candle before he himself retired. Also, unlike the rest of the family, she made no mention of the ghost in letters to her brothers, or, if she did, whatever she wrote was destroyed, either by herself or by someone else. These circumstances, together with Hetty's tendency to mischief, have been viewed, as we have already seen, by some authors as suggesting that she may in some measure have been responsible for the tappings that went on. Perhaps on these occasions she was entertaining some young man, who may actually have done the tapping — an idea which would confirm the rector's original suspicion that the noises were made by the girls' lovers.

The Wesley girls manifestly felt keenly the lack of suitable young men in Epworth. This is evident in the following verse that Hetty wrote to her sister Emilia:

> Fortune has fixed thee in a place
> Debarred of wisdom, wit and grace:
> High births and virtue equally they scorn,
> As asses dull on dunghills born;
> Impervious as the stones their heads are found,
> Their rage and hatred steadfast as the ground.
> With these unpolished wights thy youthful days
> Glide slow and dull, and Nature's lamp decays;
> Oh what a lamp is hid 'midst such a sordid race![1]

Samuel Wesley constantly determined whatever boy-friends were not in his opinion the right ones for his girls. Various young men sought the company of the beautiful Hetty, but her father apparently rejected one after another. In lines addressed to her mother she requested,

> Pray speak a word in time of need,
> And with my sour-looked father plead,
> For your distressèd daughter.[2]

Sir Arthur Quiller-Couch, in his *Hetty Wesley*, has given us a colourful picture of this extraordinary young woman. He describes her among her sisters (she was in her mid-twenties at the time) as 'Hetty of the high spirits, the clear eye,the springing gait; Hetty, the wittiest, cleverest, mirthfullest of them all.'

He goes on to state: 'If the six sisters were handsome, Hetty was glorious. Her hair, something browner than auburn, put Emilia's in the shade; her brows, darker than even dark Patty's, were broader and more nobly arched; her transparent skin, her colour — she defied the sun-rays carelessly, and her cheeks drank them in as potable gold — made Nancy's seem but a dairymaid's complexion. Add that this colouring kept its original freshness; add too, her mother's height and more than her mother's grace of movement, an outline virginally severe yet flexuous as a palm-willow in April winds, and you have Hetty Wesley at twenty-seven — a queen in a country smock and cobbled shoes, a woman made for love, and growing towards love, though repressed and thwarted.'[3]

Hetty was equally outstanding when it came to intellectual qualities. To her knowledge of English and the classical languages was added her inherited gift of poetry. Dr John Julian, editor of the *Dictionary of Hymnology*, makes the assertion: 'If she did not write hymns she showed plainly that she could have done so with a success that might have rivalled Charles's own. Mehetabel Wesley had an exquisite poetic genius.'[4] She wrote poetry and her mind ran spontaneously in a poetic vein.

It may be said of Hetty, as of her mother, that if the universities of those days had allowed women to enter, she would have proved as able a scholar as any of the Wesley men. And it is probable that had there been athletic programmes for women she would have showed herself to be proficient in that field too.

One of Hetty's chief characteristics was the passion inherent in her nature. As Quiller-Couch asserted, here was a woman 'made for love' and worthy of the finest man in the land. But, forbidden the university and denied the opportunity of obtaining suitable employment, Hetty, like her sisters, was confined to the narrow life of her home. As we think of her in her twenties, we see her feeding chickens, tending pigs and taking in hay. Indoors she transcribed for her father, but she also made certain that his tobacco and snuff were ever close at hand. And she helped her mother with the cooking, brewing and housekeeping.

Hetty manifestly loved her mother and though she nursed a steady resentment towards her father, she clearly respected him. The other sisters consented to his domination, but Hetty, although never disobedient in any outright manner, did not demonstrate the same measure of submission.

Susanna undoubtedly recognized Hetty's unusual qualities, but she also seems to have felt that this daughter needed to be checked and governed. Samuel held this opinion even more intensely.

Like many fathers of that century, Samuel believed that it was his right to control the lives of his daughters. He was not opposed to their being married—which would free him from the responsibility of supporting them — but he was concerned as to what men they kept company with, and above all, whom they married. He rightly wanted to save them from a fate like that of Sukey, who had married the foul-mouthed and heartless Richard Ellison.

The year 1724 brought a change in location for the Wesleys. In that year Samuel secured the rectorship of the parish of Wroot, a village about five miles from Epworth. Although he remained rector of Epworth, he and his family moved to Wroot and by hiring a curate to assist him he served both parishes. Wroot added some £50 to his annual income, but he spent a large part of it in paying the curate.

Ellison and Sukey rented the Epworth rectory. This arrangement frequently threw the rector and Ellison into each other's company and Samuel was constantly pained by his son-in-law's bad language. And to make matters worse, Ellison scorned Samuel's domination of his family and by his manner towards him he to some extent broke the spell the father had cast over his children. But Samuel could do little about it, for he had borrowed money from Ellison and had not been able to repay it.

Another young man was now introduced into the circle of the Wesley family. This was John Romley, the schoolteacher at Wroot. He had attended Oxford University and his father had previously served as curate at Epworth. Here was a cultivated young man close at hand and, as was to be expected, a warm friendship began to develop between him and Hetty, who was now twenty-seven.

Romley had a fine voice and he was asked to sing before a small company who had gathered one evening at the rectory. He appears to have chosen a satirical song, possibly 'The Vicar of Bray'[5], a humorous account of a clergyman who endeavoured, by constantly changing his allegiance, to retain the good will of the monarchy and thereby gain preferment. In the days of King Charles this vicar had been a fervent churchman, but quickly surrendered these principles and moved towards Catholicism when the Catholic King James came to the throne. However, when the crown was given to William of Orange he professed allegiance to the new king, to Protestantism and the Church of England. He continued of this opinion until Anne became queen, when he loudly asserted his loyalty to her and his stand in politics as a Tory. At Anne's death King George came to the throne, causing him to say,

My principles I changed once more,
And so became a Whig, sir:
And thus preferment I procured
From our faith's great Defender,
And almost every day abjured
The pope, and the Pretender.

Whether it was this song which Romley chose or some other like it, it was a stinging parody of the changes made by Samuel Wesley in his endeavours to gain preferment. On hearing the song Richard Ellison, who was no doubt present, would have been loud in his laughter and have provoked others into similar behaviour. As might have been expected, the rector was highly incensed at hearing himself ridiculed before this company of young people. He angrily ordered Romley out of the house and forbade Hetty to associate with him.

During the days that followed she obeyed, outwardly at least, but she and Romley corresponded privately. Samuel soon discovered this and decided that she must be placed somewhere where she would be well separated from Romley. Without giving Hetty the least intimation of his plan, he called on a well-to-do family, the Granthams, in the village of Kelstern, some few miles away. He offered Hetty's services as a companion to Mrs Grantham, apparently saying that she did not need to be paid.

Samuel then returned to Wroot. He told Hetty what he had done and said he was taking her to Kelstern immediately. She protested most vigorously, but he would not listen, and this time Susanna agreed with him. He drove Hetty to the Granthams' and left her there.

After some months of misery Hetty wrote to her brother John, telling him of her plight. Her letter, written on 7 March 1725, reads:

I had answered your very obliging letter long before now, only your particular enquiry into Romley's affair put me upon so melancholy a tack that you can't wonder that that so long deferred the performance. You know that my father forbade him his house on account of the old song, when you were at Wroot; since which time I have never seen Romley. He writ to me several times since, and we held a secret correspondence together, till a little while before I came to Kelstern. I desire you would not be inquisitive how the intrigue broke off; the bare mention of it is much, much worse than I can bear.

My father came to Kelstern, Christmas was twelvemonth, and proffered me to wait on Mrs Grantham. She accepted it and my father promised Mr Grantham that I should come hither before I knew a word of it. When I did know 'twas in vain for me to endeavour to persuade my parents not to send me. They were resolutely bent on my journey; so I came very much against my consent, and had far rather have gone to my grave!

Dear Jack, I think I may write freely to you, for I've such an opinion of your generosity and good nature, that you will neither upbraid me with my weakness yourself, nor betray me to those that will, I mean our family. Though I'm sensible of the great folly of complaining where the grievance admits of no remedy, yet I find that misery and complaint are almost inseparable in our sex, and I've often concealed my uneasiness to the hazard of sense and life for want of some friend to console with and advise me.

I am in a great measure careless of what becomes of me; home I would not go, were I reduced to beggary; and here I will never stay, where they tell me they would never have desired my company, only my father proffered me, and they did not well know how to refuse me; and Mrs Grantham desires me to provide for myself against May Day.

So I intend to try my fortune at London, and am resolved not to marry yet, till I can forget Romley, or see him again. Could I live without thinking, or had anything to divert my thoughts from what I don't care to think of, I might yet be easy. But here I've no company but my fellow-servants, and sometimes those that I care less for, viz. my lovers — a set of mortals who universally own me the most unaccountable woman that ever they knew. I'm condemned to constant solitude and have not been out of the town once since I came into it.

I thank you for the books you sent me, but I don't care to read the *Fair Penitent*, though I admire it vastly. The poem you desire I cannot find, and cannot write it again, because I've forgotten it, and almost everything else. So I can't desire the young lady's poetry you mentioned, though you seem to think it good, a thing almost remarkable in a woman.

Forgive my unmerciful scrawling, and think how much I value your letters, when I write now in as great a pain as I can to oblige you, and entice you to write again as soon as possible, to

Yours

M. Wesley[6]

Hetty's unhappiness at the Granthams is fully evident. Mrs Grantham had never wanted her and she had been made to feel like an interloper. Having received no wages, she had not been able to leave town, even for an hour. She had her lovers, but cared for none of them. Above all, she longed for John Romley, and this woman whose whole nature cried out for love ought never to have been separated from him. But Mrs Grantham had now asked her to leave and had set the date. She was utterly dejected and was growing desperate as she tried to decide where she could go and what she could do.

This was the situation to which Samuel Wesley, by his dictatorial methods, had reduced his beautiful and highly gifted daughter.

We have no information on Hetty's activities during the next few months. She probably went to London and stayed with her uncle Matthew and his wife, and she may well have found gainful employment.

She had stated very clearly in her letter to John: 'Home I would not go...' She was determined not to return to Wroot and be subjected again to her father's heartless domineering. Nevertheless before long — around the first of October — she did precisely what she had said she would never do: she returned to the rectory at

Wroot. Her appearance immediately moved her father and mother to horror and anger and undoubtedly covered her sisters with anguish and caused them to burst into tears. The reason? Hetty was five months pregnant.

Samuel treated Hetty as something untouchable. She later told him in a letter, 'I would have given one of my eyes for the liberty of falling at your feet,' but he would not allow so stained a thing near him. She had brought disgrace upon the name of Wesley, had broken the law of God, and her sin was evident to all. Although she was a single woman she would soon give birth, and the rectory would become the home of a fatherless child. Accordingly, to save further dishonour being thrust upon himself, his family and his parish, he must see to it that she was married, and married without delay.

Samuel had disciplined those in his parish who were guilty of fornication by forcing them to stand on the damp clay floor of the church, their shameful persons covered with a white sheet, and this act of penitence had continued for three successive Sunday mornings.[7] But on this daughter he imposed, not a temporary punishment, but a life sentence.

A journeyman plumber, William Wright, was then travelling through the district, doing whatever jobs proved available. He appeared to be industrious, but was unlearned, boorish in his behaviour and somewhat given to drink. The circumstances of the rector's meeting Wright are not known, but finding that he was unmarried, and perhaps convincing himself that he was at least honest, Samuel offered Hetty to him as a wife. And Wright, acting as though he was receiving a gift fallen from heaven, jumped at the opportunity.

Hetty was not asked if she would marry Wright. Despite her age — she was now twenty-eight — she was allowed no voice whatsoever in the matter. Although she would have agreed that Hetty must be married, and married right away, Susanna must have been shocked by the vast difference in their characters and abilities. There is probably much truth in Quiller-Couch's report that she declared, 'To think of Hetty and William Wright together makes my flesh creep.'

Each of Hetty's brothers sided with her in this matter, as did also her crippled sister Mary. John preached in his father's presence a sermon entitled 'Showing charity to sinners', and Samuel, who already was, as John said, 'inconceivably exasperated,' became still more out of patience with Hetty and now with John too. Mary is reported as standing before her father and asserting, 'Oh, sir, you are a good man! but you are seldom kind and rarely just... You are a tyrant to those you love; and now in your tyranny you are going to do what even in your tyranny you have never done before — a downright wickedness.'[8]

In spite of all these protests, the couple were quickly married. Samuel refused to conduct the marriage service for such a shameful person himself, but he sent the pair to the Rev. Joseph Hoole, rector of Haxey, and on 13 October 1735 the rite was performed. We may be sure there were no flowers, no guests and no music, and that although Wright was overjoyed, Hetty was in tears.[9]

The couple went to live with Wright's widowed father at Louth. Quiller-Couch portrays him as a nasty personality and his premises as wretchedly untidy. At any rate, conditions were very unpleasant for Hetty.

To make matters worse, soon afterwards Wright was imprisoned for a time. He went to prison in place of his father and we must assume that it was on account of the elder man's debt.

In February 1726 the baby arrived. But Hetty, who had no experience in looking after an infant, had the pain of seeing it quickly weaken and die. She had anticipated pouring out her affection on this little one, but now it was taken from her. Moreover, she regarded its death as an evidence of God's judgement upon her for her sin.

However, Uncle Matthew now came to the couple's aid and gave them £500. This enabled them to move to London, where William set up afresh in the plumbing business.

Charles Wesley had just completed his course at Westminster and was on the point of moving to Oxford. He had only seven days before leaving London and he wrote, 'Little of that time did I lose, being with her almost continually... In the little neat room she has hired did the good-natured, ingenuous, contented creature ... and I talk over a few short days that we both wished had been longer.'[10]

Susanna, on the other hand, seems to have thought Hetty's profession of repentance unreal and several months were to pass before she fully accepted her.

In a year's time Hetty was pregnant again. Still feeling that she was under divine wrath and that judgement could be averted only if she secured the forgiveness of the man of God, her father, she wrote to him. Part of her letter reads as follows:

Honoured Sir,

Although you have cast me off ... I must tell you that some word of your forgiving is not only necessary to me, but would make happier the marriage in which, as you compelled it, you must still (I think) feel no small concern. My child, on whose frail help I had counted to make our life more supportable to my husband and myself, is dead. Should God give and take away another, I can never escape the thought that my father's intercession might have prevailed against his wrath...

Forgive me, sir, that I make you a party in such happiness (or unhappiness) as the world generally allows to be, under God, a portion for two. But as you planted my matrimonial bliss, so you cannot run away from my prayer when I beseech you to water it with a little kindness... But I have come to a point where I feel your forgiveness to be necessary to me. I beseech you then not to withhold it, and to believe me to be your obedient daughter.

Mehet. Wright[11]

Samuel's reply contained the statements: 'I decline to be made a party to your matrimonial fortunes'; 'your honest husband ... I shall always think myself obliged to him for his civilities to you'; 'What hurt has matrimony done you? ... I do not know that you used to have so frightful an idea of it as you have now... Restrain your wit if you wish to write again, and I will answer your next if I like it.'[12]

Hetty had charged her father with his greatest crime — his forcing her into marriage against her will, and he could not face up to her accusation.

She replied in a very submissive manner. Here are two paragraphs of her letter:

I had not always such notions of wedlock as now, but thought that where there was a mutual affection and desire of pleasing, something near an equality of mind and person ... and anything to keep love warm between a young couple, there was a possibility of happiness in a married state; but when all, or most of these, were wanting, I ever thought people could not marry without sinning against God and themselves.

Though I cannot justify my late indiscreet letter, yet I am not more than human, and if the calamities of life sometimes wring a complaint from me, I need tell no one that though I bear I feel them. And though you cannot forgive what I have said, I sincerely promise never more to offend by saying too much; which (with begging your blessing) is all from

your most obedient daughter,

Mehetabel Wesley[13]

This was the last correspondence between Hetty and her father. We look in vain for any sign of compassion from him; it was not forthcoming and he went to his grave without the least word of reconciliation to his erring, but deeply wronged daughter. We shall look later at the closing decade of Hetty's life.

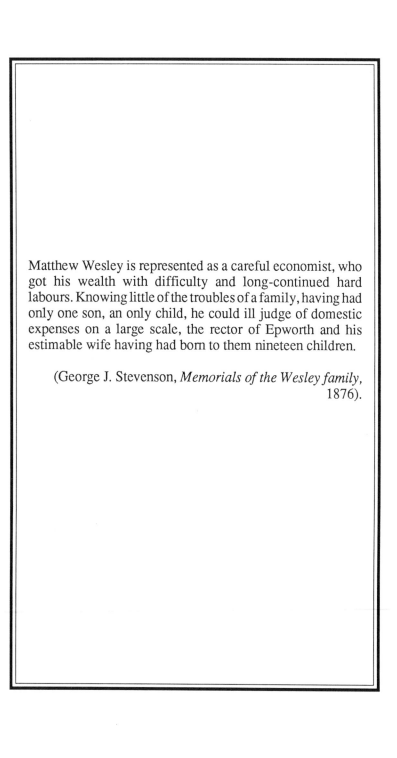

Matthew Wesley is represented as a careful economist, who got his wealth with difficulty and long-continued hard labours. Knowing little of the troubles of a family, having had only one son, an only child, he could ill judge of domestic expenses on a large scale, the rector of Epworth and his estimable wife having had born to them nineteen children.

(George J. Stevenson, *Memorials of the Wesley family,* 1876).

11

Uncle Matthew Sends
His Complaints

Matthew Wesley, like his brother Samuel, was born in a Dissenting home. Their father died at the age of forty-two and they each grew up without his guiding presence in the home. It is not known how Matthew received his education, but he probably did not attend a university. He became an apothecary, a medical practitioner with the right to prescribe and sell drugs. Residing in London, he proved so knowledgeable and industrious that he developed a large practice and acquired considerable wealth.

We have already seen that following the destruction of the Epworth rectory in 1709, two of the Wesley girls, Sukey and Hetty, went to live with Matthew and his wife, remaining there for well over a year. Matthew was an upright and honest man, but the girls noticed the difference between the easy and affluent existence in his home and the tensions and penury at Epworth. Matthew was regular in his attendance at Dissenting services and considered himself a good Christian, yet his thoughts were more taken up with professional success and the state of the stock market than with the things of God.

We must assume that Samuel at least called on this brother during his visits to London, and he may well have stayed with him, but nothing of this nature is recorded. It is also probable that Matthew's mother lived at his home during the final years of her life, but we have no definite statement that it was so.

In keeping with the practice of the well-to-do of that age, Matthew visited several of the spas of Europe. Such visits afforded him a time of holiday and the opportunity to seek to improve his health while enjoying the company of other people of affluent circumstances.

But, as year followed year, he made no attempt to visit his brother in the ministry at Epworth — that is until 1731, when he journeyed north to see him. Matthew was then about seventy years of age and semi-retired from his professional activities. He brought with him his servant, his 'gentleman's gentleman' and Susanna said in a letter to John,

My brother [Matthew] Wesley had designed to have surprised us, and had travelled under a feigned name from London to Gainsborough; but there, sending out his man for a guide to the Isle [of Axholme] the man told one his master's name, and that he was going to see his brother which was the minister of Epworth. The man he informed met with Molly [one of the Wesley daughters]... She, full of news, hurried home and told us her uncle Wesley was coming to see us; but we could hardly believe her... He rode directly to John Dawson's (the inn); but we had soon notice of his arrival and sent John Brown with an invitation to our house. He expressed some displeasure at his servant for letting us know of his coming; for he intended to have sent for Mr Wesley to dine with him at Dawson's and then come to visit with us in the afternoon. Moreover, he soon followed John home, where we were all ready to receive him with great satisfaction.

His behaviour among us was perfectly civil and obliging. He spake little to the children the first day, being employed (as he afterwards told them) in observing their carriage, and seeing how he liked them; afterwards he was very free and expressed great kindness to them all.

He was strangely scandalized at the poverty of our furniture, and much more at the meanness of the children's habit [clothing]. He always talked more freely with your sisters of our circumstances than to me: and told them he wondered what his brother had done with his income, for 'twas visible he had not spent it in furnishing his house or clothing his family.

We had a little talk together sometimes, but it was not often we could hold a private conference; and he was very shy of speaking anything relating to the children before your father, or indeed of any other matter. I informed him, as far as I handsomely could, of our losses, etc., for I was afraid that he should think that I was about to beg of him; but the girls (with whom he had many private discourses), I believe told him everything they could think on.

He was particularly pleased with Patty and one morning before Mr Wesley came down, he asked me if I was willing to let Patty go and spend a year or two with him in London. 'Sister,' says he, 'I have already endeavoured to make one of your children [Hetty] easy while she lives; and if you choose to trust Patty with me, I will endeavour to make her so too.' Whatever others may think I thought this a generous offer; and the more so because he had done so much for Sukey and Hetty. I expressed my gratitude as well as I could, and would have had him speak to your father, but he would not himself — he left that to me. Nor did he ever mention it to Mr Wesley till the evening he left us.

... Dear Jacky, I can't stay now to talk about Hetty and Patty, but this — I hope better of both of them than some others do. I pray God to bless you. Adieu.

S.W.
July 12th, 1731[1]

On his return to London, Matthew wrote to Samuel, severely upbraiding him for the condition of his children and the state of his home. In his letter he says,

The same record which assures us an infidel cannot inherit the kingdom of heaven, also asserts in the consequence that a worse than infidel can never do it. It likewise describes the character of such an one: 'He provides not for his own, especially those of his own house.'

You have a numerous offspring; you have had a long time a plentiful estate, great and generous benefactions, and made no provision for those of your own house, who can have nothing in view at your exit but distress. This I think a black account, let the case be folly, or vanity, or ungovernable appetites.

I hope Providence has restored you again to give you time

to settle this balance, which shocks me to think of. To this end I must advise you to be frequent in your perusal of Father Beveridge on Repentance, and Dr Tillotson on Restitutions; for it is not saying, 'Lord! Lord!' will bring us to the kingdom of heaven, but doing justice to all our fellow-creatures, and not a poetical imagination that we do so. A serious consideration of these things, and suitable actions, I doubt not, will qualify you to meet me where sorrow shall be no more, which is the highest hope and expectation of

Yours, etc,

Matthew Wesley[2]

Samuel must have been shocked to receive this letter. He had long told himself that the conditions in which Susanna and the girls lived did not matter. The important thing was that he had given his three sons the best education that England could provide, yet here, his own brother had overlooked that accomplishment and had castigated him for not doing better by his wife and daughters.

The rector, who had virtually never admitted himself to be in the wrong in anything, but always ascribed his faults to unavoidable circumstances, now continued that practice. He replied to Matthew in a somewhat jocular style, introducing an imaginary character and saying,

When I had read this to my friend John O'Styles I was a little surprised he did not fall into flouncing and bouncing, as I have too often seen him do on far less provocation... He stood calm and composed for a minute or two, and then desired he might peruse the letter, adding, that if the matter of fact therein were true, and not aggravated or misrepresented, he was obliged in conscience to acknowledge it, and ask pardon, at least of his family. If it were not true, he owed that justice to himself and family to clear himself, if possible, of so vile an implication.

After he had read it over he said he did not think it necessary to enter into a detail of the history of his whole life, from sixteen to upwards of seventy ... but the method he chose ... would be to make some general observations on those general accusations which have been brought against him, and then to add some balance of his incomes and expenses ever since he entered upon the stage of life.

The sum of the libel may be reduced to the following assertions:

1. That John O'Styles is worse than an infidel, and therefore can never go to heaven...

Answer. If God has blessed him with a numerous offspring, he has no reason to be ashamed of them, nor they of him, unless perhaps one of them [Hetty]. Neither does his conscience accuse him that he has made no provision for those of his own house... But has he none, nay, not above one, two, or three, to whom he has given the best education that England could afford, by God's blessing on which they live honourably and comfortably in the world? Some of them had already been a considerable help to the others, as well as to himself... There are many gentlemen's families in England who ... would be glad to change the best of theirs, or even all their stock, for almost the worst of his.[3]

By the time Samuel had written to this point he could go no further. As a result of a slight stroke some time previously, his right hand was partially paralysed, and he dictated the rest of his letter, with first Susanna and then John doing the writing.

Samuel answers Matthew's complaint that his girls, 'at their father's exit will have nothing in view but distress', by asserting that God will look after them. He then lists the various amounts he had received in the early years of his ministry and values his annual income while at Epworth at £200. He mentions the two fires, his rebuilding of the rectory and his great commentary on the book of Job, 'whereby', he says, 'he hoped he might have done some benefit to the world, and in some measure amended his fortune'.

He then attempts to set out his *Income* and his *Expenditures* in two parallel columns. He lists 'his income, about £200 per annum for near forty years, £8,000', and while he leaves six items of expenditure without attaching any amount, the four for which he provides a figure amount to merely £720. He concludes by stating, 'Let all this be balanced, and then a guess may be easily made of his sorry management. He can struggle with the world, but not with providence; nor can he resist sickness, fires and inundations.'⁴

Matthew Wesley's experience probably made it difficult for him to understand his brother's situation. While Matthew had exercised a profession that made it possible for him to acquire riches by means of true skill and untiring industry, Samuel, though equally skilful in his profession and equally diligent in his efforts, had been left in a country church, the income of which was but a fraction of that enjoyed by his brother. He had supplemented it to some extent by his writing and had tried hard to acquire a more lucrative parish, but all of his attempts to gain preferment had failed.

Samuel had made his choice to educate his sons rather than to provide for his wife and daughters. It could be argued that he might have done better to have let John and Charles work their own way through the university, as he had done himself, but he was in no sense of that mind.

Nevertheless, although we may understand Matthew's revulsion at the state of the home and the penury endured by Susanna and the girls, we should also recognize the value of Samuel's decision. We must ever bear in mind all that was accomplished through John's ministry and the spiritual wealth contained in Charles's hymns, both of which have been a tremendous blessing to countless Christians ever since. At the same time these benefits were only achieved through the difficult sacrifices made by Susanna and her daughters, as witnessed so strikingly by Uncle Matthew.

Lo, children are an heritage of the Lord; and the fruit of the womb is his reward. As arrows are in the hand of a mighty man; so are children of the youth. Happy is the man that hath his quiver full of them; they shall not be ashamed, but they shall speak with the enemies in the gate.

(Psalm 127:3-5).

Samuel Wesley, eldest son of Susanna and Samuel

12

Susanna's Children

We have seen that Susanna bore nineteen children in nineteen years. Nine of these died in infancy, but we shall now glance briefly at the careers of the ten who lived.

The first child, Samuel junior, was taken when he was only a few months old to live at South Ormsby. He attended a grammar school there (the only one of the ten to do so), but on reaching the age of fourteen he was sent to the school attached to Westminster Abbey in London. Susanna manifested her particular care for him by the series of letters she wrote to him during the ensuing months, presenting Christian doctrine and warning him of the dangers of falling into sinful ways.

At the age of nineteen Samuel entered Oxford University. He secured his Master of Arts degree, was ordained and returned to Westminster as a teacher. After twenty years he moved to Tiverton in Devonshire, where he became the headmaster of an endowed school. He was an able, scholarly teacher and was particularly gifted as a poet. He was exceptionally generous towards his parents and while at both Westminster and Tiverton he provided them with all that his salary allowed. His widowed mother was heartbroken by the death in 1739 of this son, her first-born and her chief financial support.

The second child to survive was the girl Emilia. She was ten years old when Susanna began the school in her house, but she had been under discipline and, we may be sure, instruction long before this. During the year that followed the 1709 fire, by which time she was a young woman of eighteen, Susanna kept her at home to assist her, and the two became very closely attached. A year later Susanna wrote a sixty-page treatise, *A religious conference between Mother and Emilia,* based on the Scripture: 'I write unto you, little children, of whom I travail in birth again, until Christ be formed in you.' And in her introduction she prayed, 'May what is sown in weakness be raised again in power. Written for my children.'

But Susanna's earnest efforts on behalf of the souls of her children were offset in Emilia's mind by her father's failure to provide for their bodies. Speaking of the years that followed the fire, Emilia wrote, 'I began to find out that we were ruined. Then came on London journeys, convocations of blessed memory, that for seven winters my father was at London, and we at home in intolerable want and afflictions... Thus we went on growing worse and worse; all of us children in scandalous want of necessaries for years together; vast income, but no comfort or credit with it.'[1] Thus it is evident that Emilia thought that her father's income was sufficient to afford his family a comfortable life. But instead they suffered this 'scandalous want of necessaries' and Susanna shared in this as well as her children.

During her early twenties Emilia was employed as a teacher at a girls' school in Lincoln, but after some two years, knowing her mother was in great need of her help, she returned to Epworth. While she was teaching she had owned a few possessions, but back at home she had to face the fact that such things were no longer available. She declared, 'I found what a condition I was in — every trifling want was either not supplied, or I had more trouble to procure it than it was worth. I know not when we have had so good a year, both at Wroot and Epworth, as this year; but instead of saving anything to clothe my sister and myself, we are just where we were. A noble crop has almost gone, beside Epworth living, to pay some part of those infinite debts my father has run into.'[2]

A little later Emilia spent some months living at the home of her uncle Matthew Wesley in London. While there she fell in love with a man named Leybourne and he made it appear that he was equally in love with her. But her brother Samuel, who had been at Oxford with him, stated he was not to be trusted and despite her deep affection for him the relationship was broken off.

At the age of forty, Emilia began a school for girls at Gainsborough. Here she fell in love with a man who was a Quaker, but being advised by her brothers that she ought never to marry anyone of that faith, she also ended this relationship.

In desperation Emilia married an apothecary named Harper. But his business was in difficulties and he seized whatever money she made from her school and only allowed her a pittance. He proved truly heartless and made her life miserable.

Emilia manifestly felt that it was because their father had spent so much on educating his sons that his daughters and their mother had been allowed to suffer. None the less, her brother John often assisted her and after her husband died he provided a comfortable lodging for her and her servant in London.

The next surviving child was the girl the family called Sukey. As we have seen, following the fire she and Hetty went to live with their Uncle Matthew in London and Susanna feared that, being free from the controls of home, they might feel the temptation to wander. In a letter to Sukey she said, 'You have learned some prayers, your creed, and catechism, in which is briefly comprehended your duty to God, yourself, and your neighbour. But, Sukey, it is not learning these things by heart, nor your saying a few prayers morning and night, that will bring you to heaven; you must understand what you say, and you must practise what you know... I cannot tell if you have ever considered the lost and miserable condition you are in by nature. If you have not it is high time to begin to do it, and I shall earnestly beseech the Almighty to enlighten your mind, to renew and sanctify you by his Holy Spirit, that you may be his child by adoption here, and an heir of his blessed kingdom hereafter.'[3]

Susanna certainly manifested in this letter a conviction that salvation is not something obtained by an outward performance of religious ritual, but that it requires obedience from the heart.

Susanna's brother, Samuel Annesley, had, as we saw, declared his intention of providing for Sukey after he returned from India and for years she looked forward to the fulfilment of his promise. But later he wrote saying he had changed his mind.

Stung by this sudden loss, 'she rashly threw herself,' as Susanna said, 'upon a course, vulgar, immoral man, little inferior to the apostate angels in wickedness,' Richard Ellison. She immediately began to suffer as a result of his vile behaviour and cruel actions. After some years the Ellisons' home was destroyed by fire. Ellison's temper became even more bitter and Sukey fled to London, taking her children with her. It is claimed that her husband then published an announcement of his death in the hope of enticing her out of hiding. She went into Lincolnshire to attend the funeral, only to find him alive. But she utterly refused ever to live with him again.

Ellison later lost all his cattle when his land was flooded and although he had begun with considerable riches which he had inherited he now found himself almost penniless. During his last months he attended the Methodist meetings held by John in the Foundery and there he professed to be converted.

Of Sukey herself, John was to say in 1764 that she 'was in huge agonies for five days, and then died in the full assurance of faith'.

Susanna's next child was named Mary. Due to an accident in her infancy she grew up crippled and shorter than the other girls. Apparently, but without reason, she felt herself inferior and at one time she stated, 'I have been the ridicule of mankind and the reproach of my family.' There is no record of any of the Wesleys treating her with anything but kindness, indeed, they seem to have shown an unusual affection towards her. One can only suspect that her inability to engage in physical activities on the same scale as her sisters may have caused her to feel left out and exposed to ridicule. Her outlook on life was pessimistic and she was convinced that she would never find a man who would marry her.

But she was wrong in this. In 1723 Samuel Wesley took into the rectory a tall, thin young man, John Whitelamb. He was to perform such chores as carrying wood and drawing water, but since he wrote with a good hand the rector soon started using him to transcribe his manuscript. He proved so obedient that Samuel also taught him Latin and Greek and in 1730 sent him to Oxford University. After graduating Whitelamb was ordained and became Samuel's curate at Epworth. An affection sprang up between him and Mary Wesley and in 1734 they were married. The Lord Chancellor agreed to Samuel's request that this young cleric be appointed to the parish of Wroot, whereupon the rector and his family returned to Epworth. Mary and John were manifestly in love and entered upon their duties with joy. A happy life seemed about to blossom before them, but, sad to say, within less than year, Mary died in childbirth.

Even during Hetty's darkest days this crippled sister had stood by her and now Hetty, moved with sorrow, wrote an 'Epitaph' on her, one stanza of which reads:

If savage bosoms felt her woe,
Who lived and died without a foe

How should I mourn, or how commend,
My tenderest, dearest, firmest friend?
Most pious, meek, resigned and chaste,
With every social virtue graced.[4]

When Matthew Wesley wrote his will he evidently did not know that Mary Whitelamb had recently departed this life. He left her £200.

We have already considered Hetty Wesley at some length but must now look at the later years of her life.

After her third baby died William Wright sent a note to John Wesley which ended with the sentence: 'I've sen you sum verses that my wife maid of dear lamb. Let me hear from one or both of you as soon as you think convenient.'[5]

Once more suffering a broken heart, Hetty expressed her sorrow in a poem, 'A mother's address to her dying infant'. Its last stanza reads:

Drooping sweetness, verdant flower,
Blooming, withering in an hour,
Ere thy gentle breast sustain
Latest, fiercest, mortal pain,
Hear a suppliant! let me be
Partner in thy destiny.[6]

Nothing could reveal more strikingly the difference between William and Hetty than these lines from their pens. More than once she expressed her desire to die, so heavy was her burden of sorrow.

William Wright also proved a trial in another way. He began drinking heavily, stayed away till the early hours of the morning and showed no concern about her. She wrote a poem addressed to him, in which, after mentioning his vile pastimes, she asserted,

Deprived of freedom, health and ease,
And rivalled with such things as these,
This latest effort will I try,
Or to regain thy heart, or die.
Soft as I am I'll make thee see
I will not brook contempt from thee...
I'll give all thoughts of patience o'er

(A gift I never lost before)...
Till life, on terms severe as these,
Shall ebbing, leave my heart at ease;
To thee thy liberty restore
To laugh when Hetty is no more.[7]

Hetty had certain of her poems accepted by literary magazines in London. She also had a break from her hard life when Uncle Matthew took her to Bristol and there she associated with various outstanding people.

Susanna, after showing for three or four years that she had been wounded by Hetty's sin, came around to the point where she accepted her fully and a rich affection grew once more between them, especially after the death of Samuel.

In 1739 John began holding services in a building in London called the Foundery and ten years later Hetty was attending these services regularly. She must have experienced a true work of grace within her heart for John accepted her as one of his spiritual workers. After her death he said to his sister Martha, 'I have often thought it strange that so few of my relations should be of any use to me in the work of God. My sister Wright was, of whom I should least have expected it...'[8]

Susanna's sixth surviving child was the daughter named Anne. Little is known of her till, in her twenties, she married a land surveyor, John Lambert. He is spoken of as 'a well-educated, well-read man'. Lambert came of a respectable family and succeeded well in his profession. He appears to have been upright in his manner of life, but Charles reports that at one point William Wright was corrupting him with drink. None the less there are no reports of any difficulties in Anne's marriage.

John Wesley, whose birth followed that of Anne by a year, rose to such prominence and is so widely known that he needs little comment here. But a mythology has been built up around his memory which portrays him as virtually perfect, while a more careful examination of his life reveals that though he manifestly inherited the good qualities of both his parents he also possessed some of his father's less desirable traits. Any writer who succeeds in divorcing his mind from all the legendary concepts and presents us with the true account of the life of John Wesley will render an invaluable service to mankind.

John Wesley

The next child was Martha, whom the rest of the children called Patty. She seems to have felt the family's poverty more keenly than the others and at the age of twenty-one she declared, 'When my father dies I shall have my choice of three things, starving, going to a common service, or marrying meanly.'

At the age of thirty she met a man named Westley Hall. He was a member of the Holy Club and a friend of her brothers, and like them he entered holy orders. He made a show of great piety but was in reality a weak and treacherous individual.

Soon after he and Martha met they became engaged and her heart was closely knit to him. But not long afterwards he visited Epworth and there he met her younger sister Kezia. He revealed nothing about his engagement to Martha and declared his deep attachment to Kezia. Then he claimed to have a revelation from heaven which ordered him to return to Martha. Hall and Martha were duly married and Uncle Matthew gave them £100 as a wedding gift.

Some few years after the marriage Hall became a curate in the Wiltshire village of Wooton and then in Flesherton near Salisbury. There he revealed his true character. Martha took a young woman into the house as a seamstress, but Hall seduced her. As the time of her delivery approached he fled to London. Martha ordered the servants to find a physician, but this they refused to do. Instead they informed her that her husband was the father of the child. She then went out herself and located a midwife, gave what money she had in the house to the needy girl and set out for London to find Hall. After the little one arrived Martha nursed it as tenderly as if it had been her own.

During the eleven or so years that the Halls lived at Flesherton Martha bore ten children, all but one of whom died in infancy. The surviving child, a boy, was subject to his father's uncontrolled temper. One day when the boy was three or four, Hall, in a fit of rage, thrust him into a dark cupboard and locked the door. The child screamed with fright and Martha's pleas for his release went totally unheeded till, with an authority born of desperation, she addressed her husband with the words: 'Sir, thank God that while my child is suffering to distraction a punishment he has not merited, I had not turned *your* babe out of its cradle. Now go and unlock that door!' And Hall, moved by the force of her words, promptly obeyed her.

One day Hall walked into the house carrying an infant that some other woman had borne to him. Martha immediately ordered a cradle to be brought and she looked after this child too as carefully as if it had been her own.

Hall finally threw off all pretensions of being a Christian. He became a Deist and then an atheist. He went for a time to Jamaica, taking a woman with him, but when she died he returned to England. Little more is known of him till his death some thirty years later, when, John Wesley said, 'He died ... I trust in peace, for God had given him a deep repentance.'

Martha lived to reach her eighty-fifth year. She was a gifted conversationalist and one of those with whom she sometimes discussed philosophical matters was Dr Samuel Johnson.

Charles Wesley, born in 1707, undoubtedly had the happiest married life of all of Susanna's children. Charles attended Westminster School and Oxford University and, after being ordained, went to Georgia with John. In the colony he found little but trouble and he remained there only seven months.

On his return to England he fellowshipped in a Moravian society and there he learned that his works would never save his soul. On 21 May 1738 he trusted solely in the work of Christ and he then came into the assurance of salvation. Moreover, the fountain of poetic expression that had been born within him was unlocked and hymn after hymn began to flow from his pen.

Led by George Whitefield into the task of preaching in the open air, although at first he was repulsed by so unorthodox a proceeding, he persisted and became an outdoor preacher of extraordinary power and unflagging zeal.

Charles exercised a mighty ministry. He met mob violence with undaunted courage and founded numerous societies. He was the first to carry the Methodist message to Cornwall, a county in which Methodism won amazing triumphs.

After performing his itinerant ministry for ten years, during which time he had no home of his own, Charles was married. His bride was Sarah Gwynne, the daughter of a Welsh squire. She freely gave up the affluent circumstances in which she had been brought up to become the wife of a poor evangelist. Their life together was almost entirely one of conjugal harmony and brought them both much happiness. Their two sons were musical geniuses.

From the time of his conversion till his death Charles was constantly active in composing poetry. Dr Frank Baker states, 'The figure 8,990 of his poems that I have read is close enough to nine

Charles Wesley

thousand to proclaim that "round" number as the total extent of his extant poems as he left them.'⁹ A large proportion of these poems were hymns. The whole vast quantity of poetry is rich evidence of the gift first possessed by Samuel Wesley and inherited in such abundance by his son.

Susanna's last child was the one they named Kezia. She proved rather weak as a girl and lacked the energy that characterized the rest of the family.

At the age of nineteen Kezia became a pupil-teacher in the school at Lincoln at which her sister Emilia had taught. She appears not to have had any boy-friends and in response to a suggestion from John that he knew a youth who would make a good husband for her she replied, 'It is my humble opinion that I shall live the life of a nun, for which reason I would not give one single farthing to see him this minute.'

Apparently Kezia worked at Lincoln for just her board. Needing new clothes and having no money to buy them, she returned after a time to Epworth and cared for her mother and father, both of whom were becoming enfeebled with age. Then she experienced the heartbreak caused by the false profession of love made to her by Westley Hall. As we have seen, Hall afterwards married her sister Martha.

Following her father's death and her mother's vacating of the rectory Kezia was in need of a home. She was too unwell to find gainful employment and, receiving an offer from the Halls to come and live with them, she accepted. This arrangement did not please John and he arranged for her to move to the home of a godly minister at Bexley. She could have been happy there, but the experience with Hall had a lasting effect and, as John said, 'She refused to be comforted and fell into a lingering illness which terminated in her death.'¹⁰ She was thirty-two.

Thus it is evident that the married lives of all of Susanna's children, with the exception of Charles and to some extent of Samuel and Anne, were marked by difficulty. But the opportunities that presented themselves to the girls to marry suitable men were very limited, both in number and range, and if they had been able to meet men possessing qualities similar to their own, their stories would no doubt have been very different and they would have brought to their own marriages many of the distinctive traits inherited from their mother. John was unbelievably impulsive in his choice of a partner, but had he married Grace Murray, as he desired, he would undoubtedly have known happiness in marriage.

All of the Wesley children were characterized by a force of personality and a strength of will that set them apart. These out-standing qualities no doubt made it less likely that the girls would find men fully suited to their needs. As we take our leave of Emilia, Sukey, Mary, Hetty, Anne, Martha and Kezia, we can rejoice in whatever happiness life brought to them, even as our hearts go out to those who knew so much sorrow.

Work and write while you can. You see Time has shaken me by the hand, and Death is but a little behind him. My eyes and heart are now almost all I have left.

(Samuel Wesley, aged sixty-three, in a letter to his son John).

JOB PATRIARCHA.

Frontispiece to Samuel Wesley's commentary on Job

13

Samuel Wesley's Last Years

Samuel Wesley worked on his Latin commentary on the book of Job for many years—possibly as many as twenty-five. He was studying the text in several ancient languages, and believed that when the work was completed it would sell in such numbers as to bring him considerable financial returns. These would enable him to pay his debts and would give him something to leave to Susanna when he died.

There was, however, no prospect of selling a large number of copies of such a volume, for it was in Latin and Job was not the most popular book of the Bible. His daughter Emilia showed that she realized how false was this hope when she said, 'My old belief yet remains, that my father will never be worth a groat ... and we of the female part of the family left to get our bread or starve.'[1]

Samuel is seen at his best in his relationships with his sons. At the time when he had forced Hetty into marriage with William Wright, John was in Wroot and had spoken of his father as being 'inconceivably exasperated' with her. John, however, sided with Hetty and as we saw, had gone so far as to preach a sermon in his father's hearing on 'Showing charity to sinners'. This action only made his father even more exasperated and he complained to Charles that John was 'taking her part'. But before long John showed that he was sorry for having offended his father and offered to work for him on the transcription of his manuscript. Samuel joyfully accepted his offer and told him he always knew he was good at heart.

Soon afterwards John returned to Oxford and his father wrote to him saying, 'Dear son, I am so well pleased with your present behaviour, or at least with your letters, that I hope I shall have no occasion to remember any more some things that are passed. And since you have now for some time bit upon the bridle, I'll take care hereafter to put a little honey on it as oft as I am able.'[2]

John was at that time considering entering holy orders and his father wrote to him about the serious nature of the ministerial office and urged him to broaden the scope of his studies to include such languages as Arabic and Chaldee, as well as the customary Greek and Hebrew.

Susanna also wrote to John in this regard. Her letter, written on 15 February 1725, begins, 'Dear Jacky, I was much pleased with your letter to your father about taking orders, and like the proposal well; but it is an unhappiness almost peculiar to our family that your father and I seldom think alike.'[3] She went on to say that she differed from her husband on the question of what studies were most useful to a man entering the ministry, stating that she favoured practical divinity rather than forgotten languages. But her letter closed with the words: 'I dare advise nothing.'

In 1725 John was entered as a candidate for election to a fellowship in Lincoln College and his father sought to use his influence to help him achieve it. He was also struggling to send John money to pay for his maintenance at Oxford and to meet the costs of his ordination. His self-denying actions are evident in the following letters:

Wroot, August 2nd, 1725

Dear Son,

I was at Gainsborough last week to wait on Sir J. Thorold, and shall again, by God's leave, be there tomorrow, and endeavour to make way for you in that quarter.[4]

Bawtry, September 1st, 1725

Dear Son,

I came hither today because I cannot be at rest till I make you easier. I could not possibly manufacture any money for you here sooner than next Saturday. On Monday I ... will try to prevail with your brother to return you £8 with interest. I will assist you in your charges for ordination, though I am just now struggling for life. This £8 you may depend on the next week, or the week after.[5]

Gainsborough, September 7th, 1725

Dear son John,

With much ado, you see I am for once as good as my word... I hope to send you more... God fit you for your great work! Fast — watch — pray — believe — love — endure — be happy; towards which you shall never want the prayers of

Your affectionate father,

S. Wesley[6]

In 1725 John was ordained and during the following year he was elected to the fellowship that he sought. This was more than just a recognition of his scholarship, for it afforded him an income that would average about £45 a year as long as he remained unmarried. His father was elated. But in a letter he first indicated the financial difficulties he had experienced in assisting John, saying, 'The last £12 pinched me so hard that I am forced to beg time of your brother Sam till after harvest to pay him the £10 that you say he lent you. Nor shall I have so much as that (perhaps not £5) to keep my family till after harvest... What will be my own fate before the summer be over God only knows... Wherever I am, my Jack is Fellow of Lincoln.'[7]

Samuel understandably felt a great sense of relief and happiness in knowing that John now had an income of his own and that the financial burden of maintaining him no longer rested solely on his own shoulders.

By this time, 1726, Samuel was sixty-four and he suffered a partial stroke. Its full effects are not known, but it left him with his right hand paralysed. Of course, this proved a tremendous hindrance to a writer and made him almost totally dependent on the assistance of others. Besides using any of his daughters who were still at home, he employed John Whitelamb especially to help him in this.

Samuel also gives us an insight into Susanna's condition at this time. It was worsening. Writing to John and Charles in 1727 Samuel said, 'You will find your mother much altered. I believe what would kill a cat has almost killed her. I have observed of late little convulsions in her frequently, which I don't like.'[8]

John assumed from his father's correspondence that his mother was drawing near to the close of her earthly journey. He expressed his deep concern in a letter and Samuel replied, correcting him and saying, 'We received your compliments of condolence and congratulations to your mother on the supposition of her near approaching demise, to which your sister Patty will by no means subscribe ... though she has now and then some very sick fits, yet I hope the sight of you would revive her.'[9] Samuel also reported another daughter's kindness to Susanna saying, 'Mary miraculously gets money even in Wroot, and has given the first fruit of her earning to her mother, lending her money, and presenting her with a new cloak of her own buying and making...'[10] Susanna was in fact not yet approaching her demise, but still had several years of life before her.

Two years later, however, Samuel, who by then had reached the age of sixty-six, suffered two accidents, either of which could have cost him his life. He stated in a letter to John:

> God has given me two fair escapes for life within these few weeks. The first was when my old nag fell with me, trailed me by my foot in the stirrups about six yards (when I was alone, all but God and my good angel), trod on my other foot, yet never hurt me.
>
> The other escape was much greater. On Monday week, at Burringham Ferry, we were driven down with a fierce stream and fell foul with our broadside against a keel. The second shock threw two of our horses overboard, and filled the boat with water. I was just preparing to swim for life, when John Whitelamb's long legs and arms swarmed up into the keel, and lugged me in after him. My mare was swimming a quarter of an hour, but at last we all got safe to land. Help to praise him who saves both man and beast.[11]

But although he had rescued Samuel Wesley on this occasion, Whitelamb also criticized him. In a letter to Susanna he said,

> The constant struggling with my master's temper, which they only can have a just notion of who have been shut up with

whole days in his study... His satirical wit, especially in company, was more painful to me... If this would have been almost intolerable to another, much more to me who was conscious that I served him from a principle of generosity and love, and might have expected to be treated rather like a friend than one of the meanest of servants.

The poor and wretched condition I was reduced to for want of clothes, so much worse than what I had been used to, and the universal contempt it exposed me to ... and notwithstanding my silent tears and private mourning for my wretched state, yet I never ceased heartily to pray for the prosperity and health of the family.[12]

None the less, despite Whitelamb's complaints, Samuel Wesley showed his gratitude for being rescued by sending him to Oxford University.

Two years later Samuel suffered a further accident, and this proved more serious than either of the other two. It is reported by Susanna in a letter to her son John:

July 12, 1731

Dear Jacky,

The particulars of your father's fall are as follows: On Friday, June 4th, I, your sister Martha and our maid, were going in our waggon to see the ground we hire of Mrs Knight... He sat on a chair at one end of the waggon, I in another at the other end, Matty between us, and the maid behind me. Just before we reached the close, going down a small hill, the horses took into a gallop and out flew your father and his chair. The maid seeing the horses run, hung all her weight on my chair, and kept me from keeping him company.

She cried out to William to stop the horses, and that her master was killed. The fellow leaped out of the seat and stayed the horses, then ran to Mr Wesley, but ere he got to him, two neighbours ... raised his head, upon which he had pitched, and held him backward, by which means he began to respire; for it is certain, by the blackness of his face, that he had never drawn breath from the time of his fall till they helped him up.

By this time I was got to him, asked how he did, and persuaded him to drink a little ale, for we had brought a bottle with us. He looked prodigiously wild, but began to speak, and told me he ailed nothing. I informed him of his fall. He said he knew nothing of any fall. He was as well as ever he was in his life.

We bound up his head, which was very much bruised, and helped him into the waggon again, and set him at the bottom of it, while I supported his head between my hands, and the man led the horses softly home. I sent presently for Mr Harper who took a good quantity of blood from him; and then he began to feel pain in several parts, particularly in his side and shoulder. He had a very ill night, but, on Saturday morning Mr Harper came again to see him, dressed his head, and gave him something which much abated the pain in his side.

We repeated the dose at bedtime, and, on Sunday he preached twice, and gave the sacrament, which was too much for him to do, but nobody could persuade him from it. On Monday he was ill and slept almost all day. On Tuesday the gout came... We thought at first the waggon had gone over him; but it only went over his gown sleeve and the nails took a little skin off his knuckles, but did him no further hurt.'[13]

Although Samuel tried manfully to shake off the effects of this accident he was not able to do so. He was now nearly sixty-nine and following the fall from the waggon he increasingly recognized that he was getting old.

He then began to consider what could be done for Susanna in the event of his death. He had no possessions and he realized that on his passing she would be homeless, unless he could persuade one of his sons to apply for the rectorship of Epworth. The living was in the gift of the Lord Chancellor but Samuel had reason to believe that anyone whom he recommended would prove acceptable and if one of his sons applied Susanna could remain in the rectory.

Accordingly, in 1733 he wrote to his eldest son, saying, 'Dear Samuel, For several reasons, I have earnestly desired, especially in and since my last sickness, that you might succeed me at Epworth... As for your aged and infirm mother, as soon as I drop, she must turn out, unless you succeed me; which, if you do, and she survives me, I know you will then immediately ... continue her there, where your wife and and you will nourish her, till we meet again in heaven...'[14]

Samuel junior declined the offer, however. His voice was weak, he was not the preacher that his father and his brothers were, and he felt more at home in the classroom than in the pulpit. The refusal of this son proved a severe disappointment to his father and left Susanna facing a very bleak prospect.

Meanwhile, notwithstanding his incapacitated condition, Samuel was labouring to complete his commentary on Job. Several persons had already made a financial subscription to this work and he had had a considerable portion of the book printed in London. By now this project, to which he had devoted so many years and which had given him such delight, had become a constant burden.

In 1734, when Samuel was seventy-two, since his eldest son had rejected Epworth, he made the same offer to John. However, John was very comfortable in his work at Oxford. For one thing, he was leading the Holy Club — the little band of students that had first been gathered together by his brother Charles. These men met together frequently to encourage one another in their religious devotion, to provide assistance to any who needed it in their studies and to visit Oxford's two prisons. John was also happy in his academic pursuits and his income from his fellowship was sufficient for him to live on without undue concern. Although his father wrote a lengthy letter urging him to apply for the living at Epworth, John added to the disappointment already felt by both his father and his mother by rejecting the offer.

During 1734 Samuel was laid aside by sickness. For six months he was confined to the rectory and was unable to preach or to perform many ministerial duties. Accordingly, he wrote again to John, seeking to persuade him to accept the parish, and he said of this letter, 'I urged among other things the great precariousness of my own health, and the sensible decay of my strength, so that he would hardly know me if he saw me now.'[15]

Susanna confirmed this in a letter to John: 'Your father is in a very bad state of health; he sleeps little and eats less. He seems not to have any apprehension of his approaching exit, but I fear he has but a short time to live.'[16] After having suffered constant poverty throughout her married life, she now faced the prospect of homelessness during the years of widowhood that she could see stretching before her.

Samuel's second letter and Susanna's added persuasions

apparently convinced John that he should apply to succeed his father. He wrote to his friend Thomas Broughton, curate of the chapel at the Tower of London, asking that he use his influence to help him secure this position. But early in 1735 he learned from Broughton that his application had come before the Bishop of London and that the bishop had refused him because of his undue 'strictness of life'.[17] Accordingly he now had to break this news to his dying father.

In April of the same year Susanna wrote to John and Charles urging them both to come to Epworth immediately. This, she said, would be their last opportunity to see their father alive. They hurried to Epworth and arrived to find him in his final hours of life.

John reported that, despite his very evident weakness his father frequently uttered the statement: 'The inward witness, son, the inward witness, that is the proof, the strongest proof of Christianity.' 'I cannot therefore doubt,' said John, that the Spirit of God bore an inward witness with his spirit that he was a child of God.'[18]

Charles, in a letter to his brother Samuel, reported, 'The morning he was to communicate he was so exceeding weak and full of pain that he could not, without the utmost difficulty, receive the elements, often repeating, "Thou shakest me, thou shakest me"; but immediately after receiving there followed the most visible alteration. He appeared full of faith and peace... The fear of death he had entirely conquered, and at last gave up his latest human desires of finishing Job, paying his debts, and seeing you. He often laid his hand upon my head and said, "Be steady. The Christian faith will surely revive in this kingdom. You shall see it, though I shall not."'

As the end approached, his wife and four of his children, Emilia, Sukey, John and Charles, gathered round his bed. John asked whether he was not near heaven. 'He answered distinctly,' said Charles, 'and with the most of hope and triumph that could be expressed in sounds, "Yes, I am." He spoke once more, just after my brother had used the commendatory prayer. His last words were, "Now you have done all." This was about half an hour after six; from which time till sunset he made signs of offering up himself, till my brother having again used the prayer, the very moment it was finished he expired.' [19]

So died the Reverend Samuel Wesley, M.A., on 25 April 1735, at the age of seventy-three. Charles said, 'He was buried very frugally, yet decently, in the churchyard...', beside the church to which he had devoted thirty-eight years of his industrious life. And so Susanna, his long-suffering wife, began her years of impoverished, but uncomplaining widowhood.

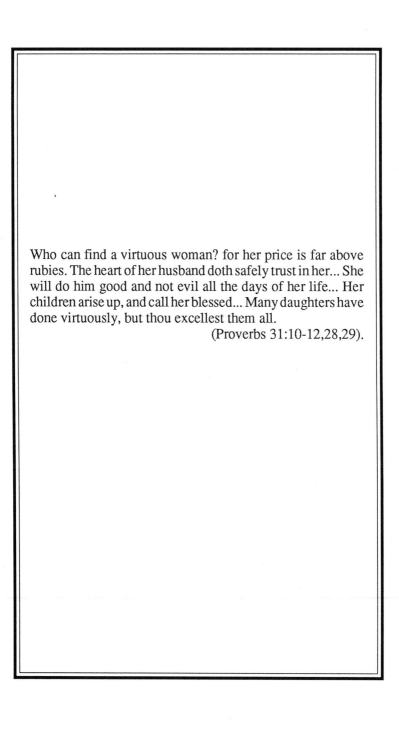

Who can find a virtuous woman? for her price is far above rubies. The heart of her husband doth safely trust in her... She will do him good and not evil all the days of her life... Her children arise up, and call her blessed... Many daughters have done virtuously, but thou excellest them all.

(Proverbs 31:10-12,28,29).

14

Susanna's Widowhood and the Grace of God

Although Susanna had revealed some weakness as she had realized that Samuel's hour of death was drawing near, she was able to face the sad event when it actually occurred with much of her usual strength. Charles tells us, 'My mother, who for several days before he died hardly ever went into his chamber but she was carried out again in a fit, was far less shocked than we expected; and told us that "now she was heard, in his having so easy a death, and her being strengthened to bear it".'[1]

And as arrangements were made for her husband's funeral Susanna also faced the grim realization that he had no possessions, that he still owed money, that his commentary on Job was not finished and that a new rector would soon be appointed to take over the parish. In only a short time, she would be obliged to move and would be dependent solely on the charity of her children. The difficult situation before her could not but have caused some alarm, even in so courageous a woman.

Her sons immediately exerted themselves on her behalf. Charles, in a letter to his brother Samuel, stated:

> We have computed the debts, and find they amount to above £100, exclusive of cousin Richardson's. Mrs Knight, her landlady, seized all her quick stock, valued at above £40, for £15 my father owed her, on Monday last, the day he was buried. And my brother this afternoon gives a note for the money, in order to get the stock at liberty to sell...
> It will be highly necessary to bring all accounts of what he

owed you, that you may mark all the goods in the house as principal creditor, and thereby secure to my mother time and liberty to sell them to the best advantage... If you take London in your way, my mother desires you will remember that she is a clergyman's widow. Let the society give her what they please, she must be still in some degree burdensome to you, as she calls it. How do I envy you that glorious burden and wish I could share it with you![2]

We must assume that Samuel applied to the society for the relief of needy clergymen's widows, but there is no evidence that she received anything from that body. But 'Samuel Wesley tells John on April 29 that he has paid £30 to save his mother, who had been arrested for debt, and £15 more to Mrs Knight "who threatened the same usage". "Mr Hutchinson and Mr Vernon have sent my mother ten guineas apiece."' Two months later, John Wesley said to Vernon, 'You have a just claim ... for continuance of your regard to my mother...'[3] Mr Vernon was one of the trustees for the colony of Georgia.

John soon finished his father's commentary on Job and had it printed. Since Samuel had dedicated it to the queen John now received permission to present a copy to her. When he 'was introduced to the royal presence, the queen was romping with her maids of honour; but she suspended her play, took the book from his hand, and said, "It is very prettily bound," and then laid it down without opening it.'

All too soon there came for Susanna the sad moment of saying farewell to Epworth and moving out of the rectory. We can imagine the feelings with which she must have packed up her few belongings and prepared to take her leave. It was undoubtedly with deep emotion that she recalled many of the experiences she had undergone there. In this house she had given birth to eleven children, six of whom she had seen buried. She was sure to think of the traumatic occasion on which Samuel had left her and her little ones and had applied for a position as a naval chaplain. And she undoubtedly called to mind the two fires, the one in which the rectory had been only partially destroyed, and the other in which the boy John had been dramatically rescued and the entire rectory had been burnt down. Here too she had conducted the school for her children, disciplining them with a firm but kind hand, training their minds and instructing them in piety as well as academics. Did she think too of Hetty, and her enforced marriage to so boorish and unsuitable a man as William Wright? These and countless other memories must have flooded her mind as she prepared to leave this house which had been her home for so long.

Susanna's sons were all willing to provide her with a home but they lacked the means to do so. John had little beside the £45 or so from his fellowship and had no place of his own in which she could live. Charles was not yet ordained and had no income apart from the small amount he earned by his tutoring. Samuel was the most able, for his school provided him with an adequate salary.

Susanna went first to stay with her daughter Emilia, who was conducting a girls' boarding school at Gainsborough. While there she wrote to John—her first letter since the loss of her husband. She began by speaking of God as the 'I AM' and then went on to say,

> I have long since chosen him for my only good, my all; my pleasure, my happiness in this world as in the world to come... Yet I do not long to go home, as in reason I ought to do. This often shocks me; and as I constantly pray (almost without ceasing) for thee, my son, so I beg you likewise to pray for me, that God would make me better, and take me at the best.

> Your loving mother,

> Susanna Wesley[4]

Life at the girls' boarding school was probably not very comfortable for Susanna. Emilia's income was not sufficient to provide more than the bare necessities of life and during the hours when school was out the place would have been filled with noise and bustle. None the less, Susanna, now a woman of sixty-seven, remained at the school for more than a year.

While Susanna was living with Emilia, John and Charles suddenly took a step which was to bring about a radical change in their lives. They left England to sail for Georgia, America's newest colony, where they intended to serve as missionaries. Methodist sentiment a century later depicted Susanna as saying, 'Had I twenty sons, I would they were all so employed,' but while that may have been her heart's desire it is to be doubted whether she actually ever used those words. She needed her sons near her and wanted them each settled in a living in England. Neither she nor they had the least idea as to when they would return, and she had reason to fear she might never see them again. Their departure was undoubtedly a cause of deep sorrow to her.

After more than a year at Emilia's school, in September 1736 Susanna went to reside with her son Samuel at Tiverton. He had always been her favourite child and his home and salary were sufficient to provide for her comfort. Although Samuel's wife had a sharp tongue and easily offended people there is no suggestion of any discord between her and her gracious mother-in-law.

However, Westley Hall apparently interfered with the harmony in the home. He told Mrs Matthew Wesley in London that there had been friction between Susanna and her son Samuel, and that she was leaving to go and live with the Halls. The spreading of this tale manifestly wounded Susanna, and Hetty, who was frequently at her Uncle Matthew's and was aware as to how the tale had come about, wrote to her mother, explaining the matter and consoling her.[5]

None the less, after nearly a year at Tiverton Susanna did leave to go and live with the Halls. Hall had not yet begun the evil practices that characterized his later years and Susanna stated, 'Mr Hall ... behaves like a gentleman and a Christian, and my daughter [Martha] with as much duty and tenderness as can be expected.'[6] She appears to have been happy throughout the time that she stayed with them.

While Susanna was with the Halls both Charles and John returned from Georgia. Her strong conviction that they owed it to her to remain in England stands out in Charles's statement that 'She vehemently protested against our returning to Georgia.'

But, in the planning of God, both of these men were about to undergo the greatest change in their lives. One of their friends, George Whitefield, who had lately left for Georgia, had been preaching in London to crowds that no church could hold. Charles had heard him, and John, on his arrival in England, learned of his outstanding success and was deeply interested. Whitefield had preached a different message from the one which the Wesleys were used to. He declared, 'Ye must be born again,' and his ministry had borne fruit in the transformation of many lives.

Whitefield's message also coincided with one the Wesleys had heard during their absence from England. While on the vessel outward bound, they had been in company with a group of evangelical Germans known as Moravians and these people —men, women and children — had set them an example of calm fearlessness amidst the fury of a raging storm at sea. Then, during their days in Georgia they had frequently been in the company of Moravians, and from them they had learned more about the gospel, the truth of 'salvation by faith'.

On their return to England the Wesleys attended a religious society that a number of Moravians also attended. John and Charles both became filled with a longing to experience the salvation by faith of which they were now constantly hearing and they yearned to receive the assurance which they were told it would bring.

Charles came into the experience of salvation first. The date was 21 May 1738, and he exultingly testified, 'I was in a new heaven and a new earth.' He tells us, 'I wrote a hymn upon my conversion,' and it was probably the one beginning,

> And can it be that I should gain,
> An interest in the Saviour's blood?[7]

Three days later, on 24 May, there came for John the now famous experience in Aldersgate Street, when he felt his heart 'strangely warmed' and felt that God had taken away his sins and saved him from the law of sin and death.[8] He then went with a company of friends to the home in which Charles was staying and they all joined in singing Charles's conversion hymn.

The Wesleys now began to declare the message of 'salvation by faith' in their preaching and in their correspondence. They wrote of their experience to their brother Samuel and he manifested his strong opposition to their 'new theology'.

Above all, they wrote of it to their mother and her replies reveal what she believed at that stage in her life concerning the way of salvation. For instance, in a letter she wrote to Charles on 19 October 1738, she said,

> Blessed be God, who showed you the necessity you were in of a Saviour to deliver you from the power of sin and Satan (for Christ will be no Saviour to such as see not their need of one), and directed you by faith to lay hold of that stupendous mercy offered us by redeeming love. Jesus is the only Physician of souls; his blood the only salve that can heal a wounded conscience.

It is not in wealth, or honour, or sensual pleasure, to relieve a spirit heavy laden and weary of the burden of sin. These things have power to increase our guilt by alienating our hearts from God; but none to make our peace with him, to reconcile God to man and man to God, and to renew the union between the divine and human nature.

No, there is none but Christ, none but Christ, who is sufficient for these things. But blessed be God, he is an all-sufficient Saviour; and blessed be his holy name that thou hast found him a Saviour to thee, my son! Oh let us love him much for we have much forgiven.

I would gladly know what your notion is of justifying faith, because you speak of it as a thing you have recently received.

Susanna Wesley[9]

Charles evidently replied that this justifying faith was indeed a thing he had only recently received. She answered:

I think you are fallen into an odd way of thinking. You say that till within a few months you had no spiritual life, nor any justifying faith.

Now this is as if a man should affirm he was not alive in his infancy, because when an infant he did not know he was alive. All then that I can gather from your letter is that, till a little while ago you were not so well satisfied of your being a Christian as you are now. I heartily rejoice that you have now attained to a strong and lively hope in God's mercy through Christ. Not that I can think that you were totally without saving faith before: but it is one thing to have faith, and another thing to be sensible we have it.

Faith is the fruit of the Spirit, and the gift of God; but to feel or be inwardly sensible that we have true faith requires a farther operation of God's Holy Spirit. You say you have peace, but not joy in believing. Blessed be God for peace! May this peace rest with you. Joy will follow, perhaps not very closely, but it will follow faith and love. God's promises are sealed to us, but not dated, therefore patiently attend his pleasure. He will give you joy in believing. Amen.

Sus. Wesley[10]

In these two letters Susanna reveals both a knowledge of the way of salvation and at the same time confusion on the subject. She declares that Christ is the only Saviour and that in order to receive him one must know one's need of him. Yet she cannot believe that Charles was 'totally without saving faith' till the event that he termed his conversion. She has no concept of being divinely remade, of becoming 'a new creation in Christ' in the new birth, but she glimpses something of the assurance of salvation for she says, 'To be inwardly sensible that we have true faith requires a farther operation of God's Holy Spirit.' In some regards she was in advance of the teachings she had long been used to, and yet in others she was in bondage to them.

Before another year had passed death again entered Susanna's family. It took her first-born, her son Samuel. Although he had been ailing for some years he had conducted his duties without fail. But 'On the night of November 5, 1739 he went to bed seemingly as well as usual, was taken ill about three o'clock in the morning and died at seven.'

Samuel had almost impoverished himself in sending money to help his father, he had assisted John during his Oxford days and had likewise aided Kezia. Devoting himself to the work of teaching, he had seldom preached, but had punctuated his life with the writing of poetry. During the following century a volume of 178 of his poems was published, drawing favourable comment from authorities on the poetry, and eight of his hymns found a place in the *Methodist Hymn Book*.

We would have expected that Susanna would be painfully distressed by the sudden loss of this son, the one she particularly loved. But in a letter to Charles she stated,

Your brother was exceeding dear to me in his life, and perhaps I have erred in loving him too well. I once thought it impossible for me to bear his loss, but none know what they can bear till they are tried... I rejoice in having a comfortable hope of my dear son's salvation. He is now at rest and would not return to earth, to gain the world. Why then should I mourn?...

It was natural to think that I should be troubled for my dear son's death because a considerable part of my support was cut off. But to say the truth, I have never had one anxious thought of such matters: for it came immediately into my mind that God, by my child's loss, had called me to a firmer dependence upon himself...

I cannot write much, being but weak. I have not been downstairs above ten weeks, though better than I was lately.[11]

About the time that Susanna wrote this letter, December 1739, her son John began using a building he had acquired in London. It was a former factory known as the Foundery. He made a large part of it into a meeting-house and a smaller section became his living quarters. Susanna said, 'Since I have been informed that Mr Hall intends to move his family to London ... I must go with them.'[12] John was now well able to provide for her and his apartment became her home for the rest of her life. While living with John she was undoubtedly as well supplied with the necessities of life as at any time since she left her father's home fifty years earlier.

Since Susanna lived virtually at John's meeting-house, as was to be expected, she began to attend his services. From the time that she had left Dissent as a girl she had known only the services of the Church of England, but she was now attending Methodist services and although Methodism was still part of the Church of England its message was different. She was aware of the change that had come in the lives and the ministries of John and Charles following their conversions in May 1738, and she now heard them declare that salvation is not the reward of works but is the gift of God 'to him that believeth'. And round about her, Sunday by Sunday, there moved a number of Methodist people who all testified with confidence that they were converted and that they were conscious of the assurance of being saved.

Westley Hall was on the verge of renouncing all relationship with Christianity but at this point he still functioned as a clergyman. At times John invited him to supply the pulpit at the Foundery and it was after one of these occasions, apparently in January 1740, when he took part in a communion service, that Susanna stated, 'While my son Hall was pronouncing these words in delivering the cup to me, "The blood of our Lord Jesus Christ which was given for thee," these words struck through my heart, and I knew that God for Christ's sake had forgiven me all my sins.'[13]

Charles Wesley was convinced that up to this point his mother had lived, to use his own words, in 'a legal night of seventy years'.

The Foundery, John's meeting-house, which was Susanna's home for the last few years of her life

In a burning desire to remove any vestiges of her long belief that she was saved by her works he wrote to her, apparently declaring that she had previously been in a lost and hell-deserving condition, and in saying such things he could be harsh and abrasive. She replied, saying,

> I thank you for your kind letter. I call it so, because I verily believe it was dictated by a sincere desire of my spiritual and eternal good. There is too much truth in many of your accusations; nor do I intend to say one word in my own defence, but rather choose to refer all things to him that knoweth all things...
>
> I am not one of those who have never been enlightened, or made partaker of the heavenly gift, or of the Holy Ghost, but have many years since been fully awakened, and am deeply sensible of sin, both original and actual. My case is rather like that of the Church of Ephesus; I have not been faithful to the talents committed to my trust, and have lost my first love...
>
> I do not, I will not, despair; for ever since my sad defection, when I was almost without hope, when I had forgotten God, yet I then found he had not forgotten me. Even then he did by his Spirit apply the merits of the great atonement to my soul, by telling me that Christ died for me.[14]

How are we to view this letter? Is Susanna stating that she did not become a true believer for the first time in the experience at that communion service, but that she had already known Christ as her Saviour for many years? Quite possibly this is her meaning. She honestly admits that she 'had lost her first love', but she also declares that God had brought her back to himself.

There is really no need for us to attempt to decide at what point Susanna was converted. Rather we may rejoice in the evidence that she had probably known the Lord for a long time and in the certainty of salvation to which she manifestly came as the result of this experience late in her life.

Susanna was now called upon to witness another death in her family. She had recently buried her first-born and now she attended the funeral of her last-born. Her youngest daughter Kezia, who had never been strong and who had suffered heartbreak when the profession of love made to her by Westley Hall had proved to be false, passed away in March 1741. 'Full of thankfulness, resignation and love, without pain or trouble, she commended her spirit into the hands of Jesus, and fell asleep.'

Susanna's own life was now likewise drawing to its close. Although many think of her as having always been a robust, healthy woman, such a concept is the very opposite of the truth. Her daughter Emilia spoke of her as repeatedly enduring suffering, 'occasioned by want of clothes or convenient meat'. And she herself said, 'I have many years suffered much pain and great bodily infirmities.' Yet she could also say, 'Those very sufferings have, by the blessing of God, been of excellent use, and proved the most proper means of reclaiming me from a vain conversation; insomuch that I cannot say I had been better without this affliction, this disease, this loss, want, contempt or reproach. All my sufferings ... have concurred to promote my spiritual and eternal good.'[15]

John's ministry took him away from home much of the time, but three of Susanna's daughters lived in London and one of them could always be with her. During July 1742, John was in Bristol, but he received a note from one of his sisters, telling him that his mother was near death. He rode post-haste to London and found her, he said, 'on the borders of eternity. But she had no doubt or fear; nor any desire but (as soon as God should call) "to depart and to be with Christ".'

The following day the daughters Emilia, Sukey, Hetty, Anne and Martha all came to John's apartment and gathered in prayerful solemnity around her bed. John's *Journal* continues: 'I sat down on the bedside. She was in her last conflict; unable to speak, but, I believe, quite sensible. Her look was calm and serene, and her eyes fixed upward, while we commended her soul to God. From three to four the silver cord was loosing and the wheel breaking at the cistern; and then, without any struggle, or sigh or groan, her soul was set at liberty. We stood around the bed, and fulfilled her last request, uttered a little before she lost her speech, "Children, as soon as I am released, sing a psalm of praise to God."'[16]

What did they sing? We are not told, but one hymn which would have been very appropriate was the one written by her son Charles that begins:

Happy soul, thy days are ended,
All thy mourning days below;

Go, by angel bands attended,
To the sight of Jesus go!
Waiting to receive thy spirit,
Lo! the Saviour stands above;
Shows the purchase of his merit,
Reaches out the crown of love.

John also reports the funeral service. He says, '*Aug. 1, Sunday.* Almost an innumerable company of people being gathered together, about five in the afternoon I committed to the earth the body of my mother, to sleep with her fathers. The portion of Scripture from which I afterwards spoke was, "I saw a great white throne, and him that sat upon it, from whose face the earth and the heaven fled away; and there was found no place for them. And I saw the dead, small and great, stand before God, and the books were opened; and the dead were judged out of those things which were written, in the books, according to their works." It was one of the most solemn assemblies I ever saw, or expect to see on this side of eternity.'[17]

The interment was in the Bunhill Fields cemetery where such eminent Christians as John Bunyan, John Owen and Isaac Watts are also buried. The stone placed over the grave bore the inscription:

Here lies the body

of

MRS SUSANNA WESLEY

The youngest and last surviving daughter of

Dr Samuel Annesley

In sure and steadfast hope to rise
And claim her mansion in the skies,
A Christian here her flesh laid down,
The cross exchanging for a crown.

True daughter of affliction, she,
Inured to pain and misery,
Mourned a long night of griefs and fears,
A legal night of seventy years.

The Father then revealed his Son,
Him in the broken bread made known;
She knew and felt her sins forgiven
And found the earnest of her heaven.

Meet for the fellowship above,
She heard the call, 'Arise my love!'
'I come,' her dying looks replied,
And lamb-like as her Lord she died.[18]

So passed from this life the soul of Susanna Annesley Wesley on 23 July 1742. She was in her seventy-fourth year.

We may well rejoice in Mrs Wesley's Christian description of death as being 'released'! For her there was no fear, no mystery, no darkness. It meant rather a happy setting free from care, from pain and trial, the rending of the bonds that had bound her to the realm of time and sense. She has passed through the valley of the shadow of death, led by her tender and all-knowing Shepherd, and now, though loved ones mourn that she is 'absent from the body', her soul has entered the unspeakable rejoicing of being 'for ever with the Lord'!

Though Susanna had nothing of earth's goods to leave to her children, she possessed many qualities of character that she passed on to each of them, in varying measure.

She had set apart an hour each day, apparently from six to seven in the evening, to be alone with God. During that time she read the Scriptures, meditated and prayed, and she allowed virtually nothing to prevent her from fulfilling this practice. In doing so, she set an example that her children could never forget.

The patience with which she bore the trials of her life — the domineering by her husband, the family's constant poverty and her several disappointments — was a remarkable feature of her character and it became evident in turn in each of the girls. The same quality was manifest in the ministries of John and Charles, as they repeatedly faced the violence of outraged mobs, yet would return the next day to declare the gospel to the same people, and continued to do so till they had won many of them to Christ.

Susanna had none of the wit that was frequently displayed by her husband, but she had about her a sincerity that governed all her actions and gave a definite purpose to her life. Similarly, although we are not given any information as to what education she received as a girl, we have seen that by the time she reached maturity she possessed a wide vocabulary, used the English language with precision and had a knowledge of theology superior to that of many ministers.

Although these qualities, in varying degrees, were passed on to all of Susanna's children, mankind has especial reason to be thankful that her sons Charles and John possessed them. We may all rejoice in the wealth of Christian song made available in the hymns composed by Charles, as well as in the masterly evangelistic career of John, culminating in his organizing of the Methodist Church. But although certain of these abilities were derived from their father, Samuel, it was especially from their mother, Susanna, in the providence of God, that they inherited the qualities which enabled them to achieve so much.

Well may all, even as many as know the name of Wesley, remembering Susanna's wealth of knowledge, her rare patience and self-sacrificing goodness, obey the scriptural injunction to 'rise up and call her blessed'!

Select Bibliography

Baker, Frank. *Charles Wesley as revealed in his letters,* Epworth, London, 1948.

Baker, Frank. *Charles Wesley's verse,* Epworth, London, 1964.

Dallimore, Arnold. *A heart set free: the life of Charles Wesley,* Evangelical Press, 1988.

Edwards, Maldwyn. *Family circle,* Epworth, London, 1949.

Fitchett, W. H. *Wesley and his century,* Briggs, Toronto, 1906.

Flint, Charles Wesley. *Charles Wesley and his colleagues,* Public Affairs Press, Washington, D.C., 1957.

Green, V. H. H. *The young Mr Wesley,* Edward Arnold, London, 1961.

Kirk, John. *The mother of the Wesleys,* Jarrold, London, 1868.

Quiller-Couch, A.T. *Hetty Wesley,* Harper, London, 1903.

Ryle, J. C. *Christian leaders of the eighteenth century,* Banner of Truth, Edinburgh.

Stevenson, George J. *Memorials of the Wesley family,* Partridge, London, 1876.

Tyerman, Luke. *The life and times of the Rev. John Wesley, M.A.,* Hodder & Stoughton, London 1880.

Tyerman, Luke. *The life and times of the Rev. Samuel Wesley, M.A.,* Simpkin, Marshall, London, 1866.

Wesley, John. *The Letters of,* ed. John Telford, Epworth, London, 1931.

Wesley, John. *The Journal of,* ed. Nehemiah Curnock, Epworth, London, 1938.

References

Chapter 1
1. George J. Stevenson, *Memorials of the Wesley family,* Partridge, 1876 (hereafter referred to as 'Stevenson'), p.158.
2. John Kirk, *The mother of the Wesleys,* Jarrold, 1868 (hereafter referred to as 'Kirk'), p.5.
3. *Ibid.,* p.20.
4. *Ibid.,* p.16.
5. *Ibid.,* p.13.
6. Stevenson, p.160.
7. *Ibid.,* p.193.
8. Kirk, p.32.

Chapter 2
1. John Dunton, *The life and errors of John Dunton,* London, 1818 (hereafter referred to as 'Dunton'), p.3.
2. Luke Tyerman, *The life and times of the Rev. Samuel Wesley, M.A.,* Simpkin Marshall, 1866 (hereafter referred to as 'Tyerman'), p.318.
3. *Samuel Wesley's Autobiography,* Ms RAWL. C. 406, Bodleian Library, Oxford University (hereafter referred to as '*Autobiography*'), p.1.
4. *Ibid.*
5. *Ibid.*
6. *Ibid.,* p.2.
7. *Ibid.*
8. *Ibid.*
9. *Ibid.,* p.3.
10. *Ibid.*
11. Kirk, p.35.
12. *Autobiography,* p.3.

Chapter 3
1. *Autobiography*, p.3.
2. *Ibid.*
3. *Ibid.*, p.4.
4. *Ibid.*
5. Eighty-four of the questions answered by Wesley are listed by Tyerman, pp.81-2.
6. *Ibid.*, p.127.
7. *Autobiography*, p.4.
8. Tyerman, p.194
9. Kirk, p.67.

Chapter 4
1. Kirk, p.79.
2. Tyerman, p.249.
3. Stevenson, pp.79-80.
4. *Ibid.*, p.81.
5. *Arminian Magazine*, 1784, p.606.
6. Tyerman, p.253.
7. *Manchester Guardian*, 2 July 1953.
8. *Ibid.*
9. *Ibid.*, 3 July 1953
10. *Proceedings of the Wesley Historical Society*, XXIX, p.55.
11. *Manchester Guardian*, 3 July 1953.
12. *Ibid.*

Chapter 5
1. Stevenson, p.168.
2. *Ibid.*, p.163.
3. *Ibid.*
4. *Ibid.*, p.164.
5. *Ibid.*, p.165.
6. *Ibid.*

Chapter 6
1. Tyerman, p.291.
2. Stevenson, pp.89-90.
3. *Ibid.*, p.90.
4. *Ibid.*, p.199.
5. Kirk, pp, 129-30
6. *Ibid.*, p.109.
7. *Ibid.*
8. Stevenson, pp. 106-7.
9. *Ibid.*, p.107.
10. *Ibid.*, pp.95-6

Chapter 7
1. Kirk, p.85.
2. Stevenson, p.195.
3. *Ibid.*, p.197.
4. Tyerman, p.349.
5. *Ibid.*, p.358.
6. The 'Old Jeffrey' affair is fully reported in Tyerman, pp. 348-64.
7. W. H. Fitchett, *Wesley and his century*, Briggs, 1906, p.40.

Chapter 8
1. Stevenson, pp. 175-6
2. *Ibid.*, p.182.
3. *Ibid.*, p.184.
4. *Ibid.*, p.185.
5. *Ibid.*, p.203.
6. *Ibid.*, p.204.
7. *Ibid.*
8. *Proceedings of the Wesley Historical Society,* 1898.
9. Stevenson, pp.96-7
10. *Ibid.*, p.101.

Chapter 9
1. Stevenson, pp. 198-9.
2. *Ibid.*, pp. 199-200.
3. *The Letters of John Wesley,* (standard edition), vol. 1, p.8.
4. *Ibid.*, p.7.

Chapter 10
1. Stevenson, p.265.
2. *Ibid.*, p.299.
3. Sir Arthur Quiller-Couch, *Hetty Wesley,* Harper & Bros, 1903 (hereafter referred to as 'Quiller-Couch'), pp.35-6.
4. John Julian, *The Dictionary of Hymnology,* article 'Hetty Wesley'.
5. 'The Vicar of Bray', anonymous, *c.*1720.
6. Letter in the *Methodist Archives,* Rylands University, Manchester. Before the process of photocopying was available certain authors assumed that this letter was written by Hetty's sister Martha.
7. Kirk, p.117.
8. Quiller-Couch, p.183.
9. The author expresses his thanks to Dr Charles Baker for several of the facts here reported in the matter of Hetty Wesley. Dr Baker researched the subject in visiting several churches and archives in England.
10. Frank Baker, *Charles Wesley as revealed in his letters,* Epworth, 1948, p.8.

11. Quiller-Couch, pp. 256-7
12. *Ibid.*, p.257.
13. *Ibid.*, pp.258-60.

Chapter 11
1. Stevenson, pp. 38-40.
2. *Ibid.*, pp. 40-41.
3. *Ibid.*, pp. 41-2
4. *Ibid.*, p.44.

Chapter 12
1. Stevenson, p.263.
2. *Ibid.*, p.264.
3. *Ibid.*, p.281.
4. *Ibid.*, p.293.
5. *Ibid.*, p.309.
6. *Ibid.*, pp.309-10.
7. *Ibid.*, p.307.
8. John Wesley, *Letters*, vol. IV, p.156.
9. Frank Baker, *Charles Wesley's verse*, Epworth, 1963, p.10.
10. John Wesley, *Letters*, vol. V, p.112.

Chapter 13
1. Stevenson, p.267.
2. *Ibid.*, p.119.
3. *Ibid.*, p.131.
4. *Ibid.*, p.122.
5. *Ibid.*, p.123.
6. *Ibid.*, p.124.
7. *Ibid.*, p.125.
8. *Ibid.*, p.128.
9. *Ibid.*
10. *Ibid.*, p.129.
11. *Ibid.*
12. *Proceedings of the Wesley Historical Society*, June 1960, p.129.
13. Stevenson, p.134.
14. *Ibid.*
15. *Ibid.*, p.147.
16. *Ibid.*, p.207.
17. Luke Tyerman, *The life of John Wesley,* Hodder & Stoughton, 1880, vol. 1, pp.102-3.
     The Rev. V. H. H. Green, D.D., Fellow and Senior Tutor at Lincoln College, Oxford University, says in his *The Young Mr Wesley* (Edwin Arnold Ltd, 1963, p.246), 'It seems ultimately that John Wesley intimated

that he would be willing to take the living (which was in the gift of the Lord Chancellor), but by that time it had been offered to and accepted by Samuel Hurst.'

18. Tyerman, p.444.
19. Stevenson, pp. 149-50.

Chapter 14
1. Stevenson, p.150.
2. *Ibid.*
3. John Wesley, *Letters,* vol. 1, pp.203, 228.
4. Stevenson, p.218.
5. Letter by Hetty Wesley to her mother (undated) in *Methodist Archives,* Rylands University, Manchester.
6. Stevenson, p.367.
7. Charles states that Luther was dealing with the Scripture, 'who loved me and gave himself for me,' and the repeated use of these pronouns in the hymn strongly suggests that this was the one Charles composed on this occasion.
8. 24 May 1738 was universally accepted as the date of John's conversion till a Roman Catholic writer, Maxim Piette, stated that his conversion had taken place when he was ordained in 1725. But in 1725 Wesley had no understanding of the truth of salvation by faith and throughout his life he spoke of 24 May 1738 as 'the day of my conversion'.
9. Stevenson, p.217.
10. *Ibid.,* pp. 217-8
11. *Ibid.,* p.218.
12. *Ibid.,* pp. 215-6.
13. *Ibid.,* p.213.
14. *Ibid.,* pp. 220-21.
15. Kirk, pp. 230-31.
16. John Wesley, *Journal,* vol. 3, pp.29-30.
17. *Ibid.,* pp. 30-31.
18. Stevenson, p. 227.

Index